ECHOES ACROSS SEYMOUR

TAKaya
seaspan

ECHOES ACROSS SEYMOUR

A History of North Vancouver's Eastern Communities Including Dollarton and Deep Cove

JANET PAVLIK • DESMOND SMITH • EILEEN SMITH

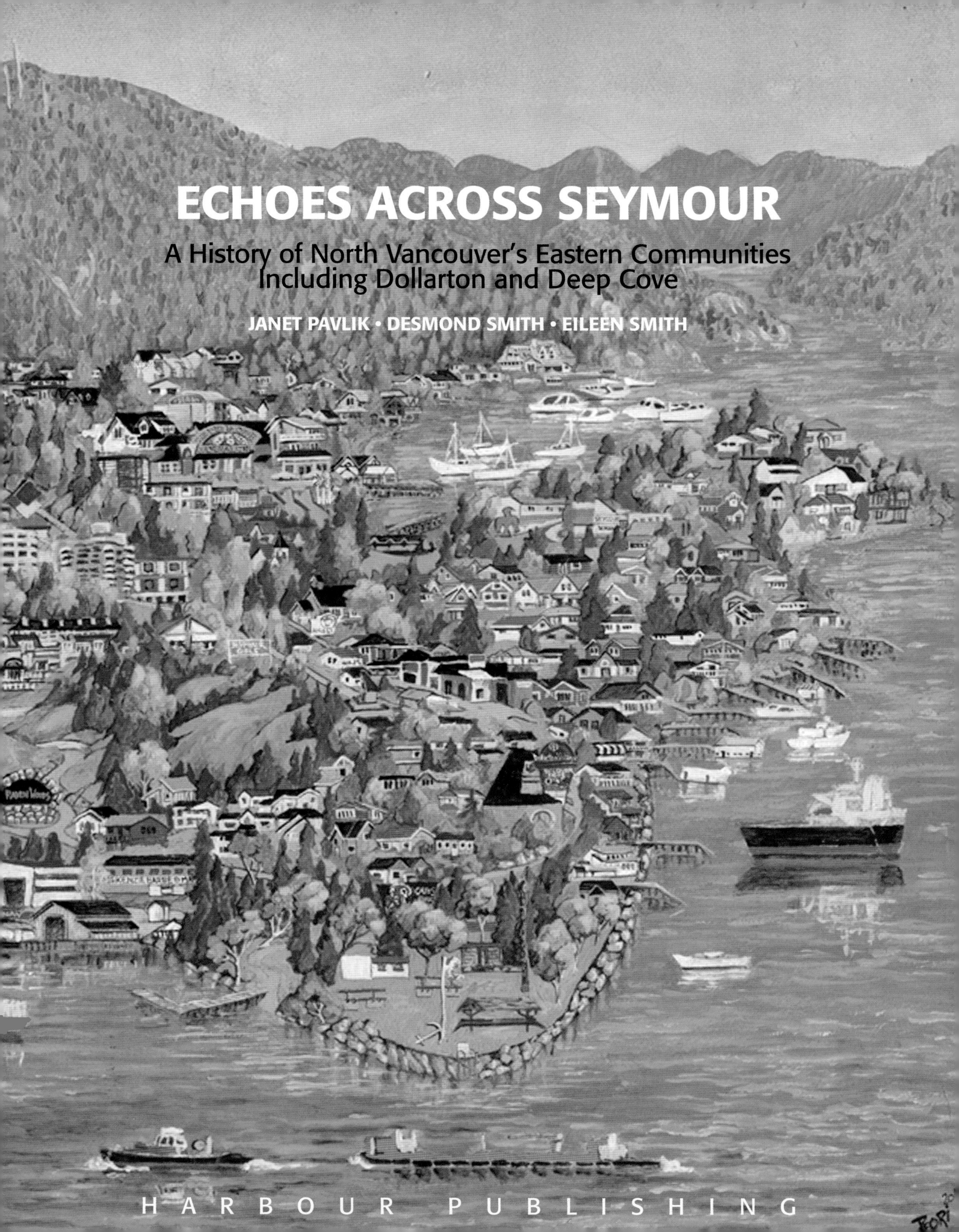

HARBOUR PUBLISHING

1 2 3 4 5 — 16 15 14 13 12

Harbour Publishing Co. Ltd.
P.O. Box 219, Madeira Park, BC, V0N 2H0
www.harbourpublishing.com

Cover and title page artwork: *Morning Over Seymour* by Cristina Peori, 4584
Cover design: Anna Comfort O'Keeffe
Text layout and design: Martin Nichols
Editor: Margaret Tessman
Index: Tyler Laing
Printed and bound in China
The publisher acknowledges the cooperation and assistance of Deep Cove Heritage Society

Special acknowledgement for the generous support of Government of Canada's New Horizons for Seniors Initiative, The Arts Office of North Vancouver, Pacific Arbour Retirement Communities—whose generous support made it possible to print the book in full colour, Bruce and Janine Coney of the *Deep Cove Crier*, Terry Peters and Mike Wakefield of the *North Shore News*, the District of North Vancouver.

Photography credits: All numbers refer to the Deep Cove Heritage Society archives unless otherwise credited. "DCHS" indicates photographs that are part of the Society's exclusive collection. Uncredited photographs are by Eileen Alway Smith. Every attempt has been made to identify and credit sources for photographs and the publisher appreciates receiving any additional information.

Harbour Publishing acknowledges financial support from the Government of Canada through the Canada Book Fund and the Canada Council for the Arts, and from the Province of British Columbia through the BC Arts Council and the Book Publishing Tax Credit.

Library and Archives Canada Cataloguing in Publication

Pavlik, Janet, 1939–
Echoes across Seymour : a history of North Vancouver's eastern communities including Dollarton and Deep Cove / by Janet Pavlik, Desmond Smith and Eileen Smith.
Includes bibliographical references and index.

ISBN 978-1-55017-588-2

1. North Vancouver (B.C. : District)—History. 2. Deep Cove (B.C.)—History. 3. Dollarton (B.C.)—History. I. Smith, Desmond, 1934–. II. Smith, Eileen (Eileen Mary Alway), 1947–. III. Title.
FC3849.N67P38 2012 971.1'33 C2012-900639-4

Contents

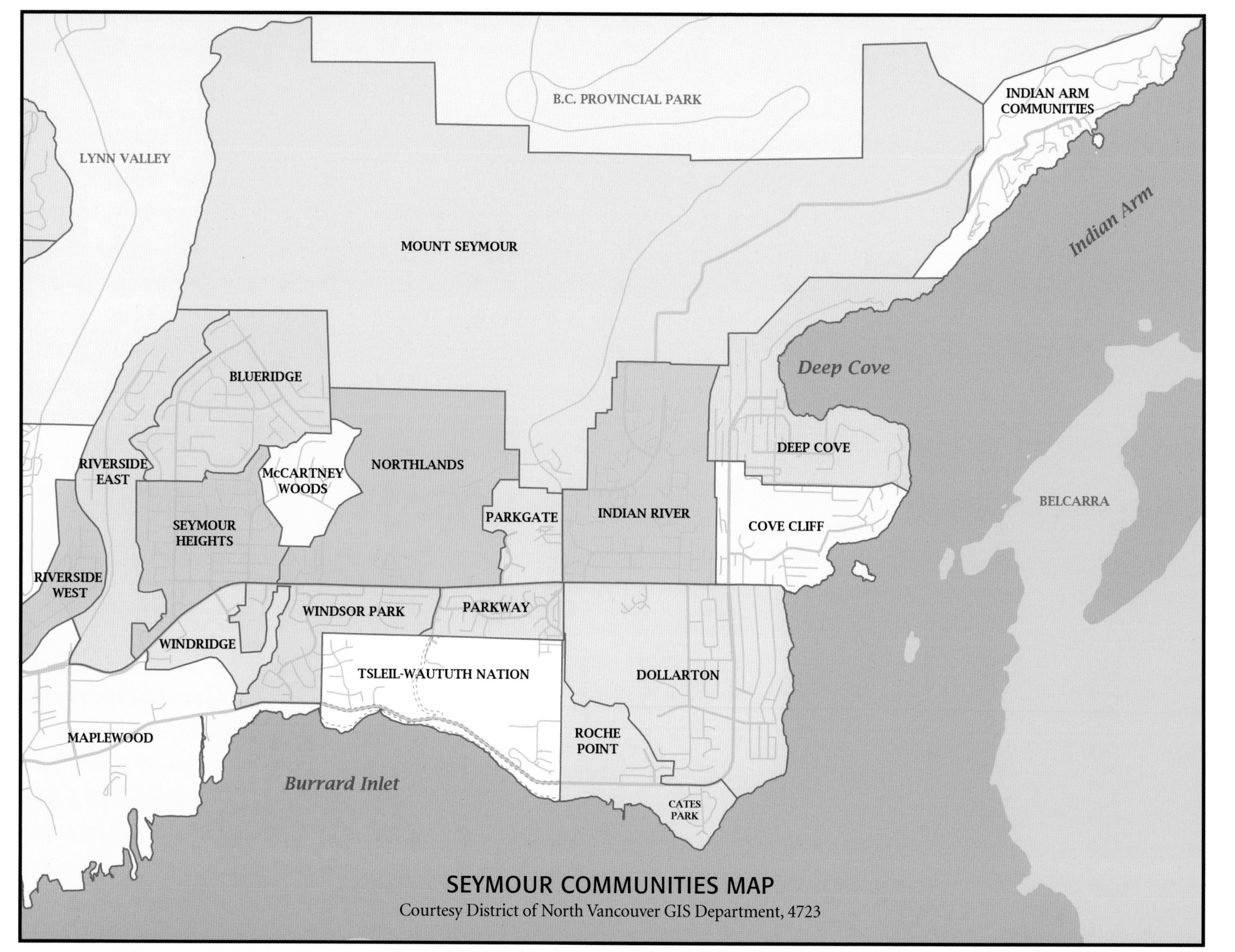

SEYMOUR COMMUNITIES MAP

Courtesy District of North Vancouver GIS Department, 4723

Community history books such as *Echoes Across Seymour* provide us with personal and unique insights into the character of the places in which we live. They are labours of love that take years to complete, and draw on the energy of a small and committed group of people.

The common passion that pulls people together on projects such as *Echoes* flows from a nostalgia to remember and document the events and people of the past. But this book is also a thank you to those who came before us and have given their time, labour and often their names to create the Seymour of today.

This book is timeless and will be read and enjoyed by our children and grandchildren and help them appreciate how our community and families changed over the years.

You will find throughout the pages of this book, a strong sense of how nature shapes and complements our lives. Seymour is a magical place where stars and forest, sea and city, mountain and stream, wildlife and humanity all strive to find balance.

So thank you to Janet, Eileen, Desmond and so many others who have put their time and passion into this book. You offer us a timeless gift.

And to you the reader, take your time and enjoy a journey through Seymour. And remember that this book is really about all of us. *Echoes* is a love story about people, landscapes and time.

Richard Walton, Mayor
District of North Vancouver

Acknowledgements

Thanks to the Team

Echoes Across Seymour is the result of a long trek across the Seymour area and a collaboration of the people of the neighbourhoods of Seymour. Thanks go to the Deep Cove Heritage Society for backing this project that has provided invaluable records, interviews, and photo material for their archives. Thanks also go to Bruce Coney of the *Deep Cove Crier* for his encouragement and support. The intent of the book is to record changes in the area over the last fifty to sixty years, with the birth of new neighbourhoods, services and facilities.

Headed up by Janet Pavlik, the team included many local residents. We were very fortunate when retired North Vancouver District planner Desmond Smith became involved. He supplied the facts on topics relating to the District and we are grateful for his contributions and insightful introductions to each neighbourhood.

Thanks also go to Dorothy Smith for her computer work; Eileen Smith, whose photography, research, scanning and childhood memories make the book come alive; Michael Smith for his ever-ready support; Adam Wilson for early design layout; Whitney Spearing, research assistant; Shelley Harrison Rae for her editorial skills; Vickie Boughen, coordinator of the Deep Cove Heritage office, and assistant Carmen Harrington; Nicholas Boughen, our pilot who flew over the Seymour area while Vickie took aerial photos; Gail Hanlon for transcribing interviews; Elaine Oakes, District of North Vancouver Records; Ray Eagle for his Seymour Planning Association report; and artist Cristina Peori for her delightful cover depicting the Seymour area.

The following local residents agreed to be interviewed and shared their personal albums with us: Florence Allardice, Suzanne Allardice, Jane Allen, Elizabeth Austin, Carole Badgely, Dick Baker, Kit Baker, Kerry Baxter, Don Bell, Hazel Best, Clara Bliss, Ann Booth, Peggy Cardno, Trevor Carolan, Bev Champion (nee Graves), Larry Chute, Lynda Dalton, Merrilee Davis, Richard de la Mare, Alex Douglas, Ray Eagle, Nora Eckland, Betty Edge, Sheila Findlater, Bob Garries, Bill Gaston, Artie George, Leonard George, Gillian Hansen, Sherril Hardy, Bill Hayden, Reverend Ed Hird, Sharon Hogan, Diana Howard, Damian Inwood, Rosemary Kenning, Donna Kriston, John Ladd, Butch Lima, Shirley and Bruce Macdonald, Jacquie Morgan, Pat Morrice, Jack Mosely, Wayne Nemith, Lynn Nicely (nee Elliot), Dirk Oostinde, Bev Parslow, Jimmy Pattison, Barb Phillips, Wendy Rasmussen, Audrey Routledge, Anne Scott, Eileen Smith, Wayne Smith, Michael Thorpe, Bill Towland, Mel Turner, Wanda Waldock, Jordan Welsh, Ron Yen and Heritage Committee members Marilyn Myers, Barry Dixon, Tom Kirk and Pat Morrice. Over four years so many people have touched and contributed to the melding of ideas for this book, including my husband, John Pavlik, who claims he has been sorely neglected during this time! We thank you all.

The majority of information in this book was offered as memories by residents. The stories and information were verified to the best of our abilities, but this book is not intended to be a volume of hard facts. If in reading this book you find that we got something wrong, we would appreciate you sending your recollections or facts to our website. We hope that there will be an ongoing dialogue there for many years to come.

Echoes Across Seymour was compiled by the Deep Cove Heritage Society with the initial help of a grant from the Government of Canada's New Horizons for Seniors program, The Arts Office North Vancouver and Pacific Arbour Retirement Communities.

The Story of the Deep Cove Heritage Society

by Janet Pavlik, who was there from the start

I guess the real beginnings of what we know today as the Deep Cove Heritage Society came in 1970 when my husband John and I and our children Misha and Paul moved to Deep Cove. Anxious to find out more about the Seymour area, I joined the Deep Cove Community Association and John joined the Mount Seymour Lions Club. I quickly discovered that very little information was available through the North Vancouver Museum and Archives.

I was elected publicity chairman for the Community Association and began talking to long-time residents and collecting their photos and stories. Eventually I interviewed many of them on a community TV program called *The Early Days of Deep Cove*, which ran in 1974–75. I also wrote a weekly column for the *Citizen* newspaper called "Around Deep Cove," and kept it going until the 1980s.

My travel business was growing and Pavlik Specialized Tours took up all my time. I kept the photos and archival material stored in our basement as I had a dream that eventually there would be a heritage group of our own in the community. Bev Parslow, a

Deep Cove Heritage members, 2008. Clockwise from left: Vickie Boughen, Janet Pavlik, Pat Morrice, Tom Kirk, Rosemary Kenning, Arthur Coverdale, Lynn Thornley, Hazel Best, Betty Edge, Vivienne Coverdale, Eric Morter, Audrey Grisdale, Eileen Smith, Lisa Kennedy. Photo by Michael Smith, 3283

teacher at Burrard View Elementary School, shared the vision. He also collected old photos in a makeshift office under the stairs at the school.

In 1985 Seycove Community School opened. Every group in the area was vying for space and we had great hopes. I decided to hand over the Heritage material to Linda Moore, Seycove Community School coordinator. She was working to acquire grant funding to establish the Seymour Art Gallery and agreed to include the plight of heritage in her application. The successful appeal made it possible to hire a gallery coordinator, Sherrill Hardy, and a museum curator, Yvonne Prudek.

Yvonne set up an office on Gallant Avenue and organized the first heritage group. At the time, heritage was part of the Deep Cove/Dollarton Community Programs Society. Later that year the Seymour Art Gallery and Archives was born and their first exhibition featured Yvonne presenting a history on Deep Cove and the surrounding communities.

The Seymour Art Gallery flourished, the heritage group grew and in 1986 the archives became the Deep Cove and Area Heritage Association. Early volunteers included Jim and Saundra Keayes, Jim and Gail Huzel, Robin Cameron, Ingrid Baxter, Collean Cosgrove, Barbara Edgeler, Finn and Eileen Ohrling, Steve and Connie Flett, Dorothy Dobson and others. The list in 1987 showed thirty-five volunteer positions.

A huge achievement in 1988–89 was the publication of *Echoes Across the Inlet*, spearheaded by Dawn Sparks, Martha Border and Damian Inwood. Many locals were interviewed and the archives expanded with all the new material. The heritage group had become a vibrant part of our community and was holding fundraising events, presentations, school programs and seniors' programs.

In 1992 we moved into new premises in the Deep Cove Cultural Centre. Although the space is small the location is great and our good working relationship with the Seymour Art Gallery, Deep Cove Stage and First Impressions Theatre is very valuable.

Damian Inwood headed up the group as president for many years and with able assistance from Joan Athey promoted *Echoes Across the Inlet* at every community opportunity. Debbie Leskiw became a part-time coordinator and kept the office open. Subsequent coordinators include Jackie Gore, Mary Johnson, Eileen Smith, Shelley Harrison Rae and Misha Wilson. Today Vickie Boughen heads up the office.

Past presidents include Damian Inwood, Donna Serviss, Pat Henderson, Janet Pavlik and Tom Kirk. Barry Dixon is our current president. Pat Morrice has been on the executive since the beginning.

In 1999 Damian Inwood and I produced First Light Over the Cove, a celebration breakfast to welcome the new millennium. This successful event brought attention to our heritage plaque located in the park adjacent to the cultural centre.

In 2000 we became the Deep Cove Heritage Society (DCHS). The perseverance of treasurer Eric Morter enabled us to become a non-profit society with fundraising opportunities, permission to apply for grants and issue tax receipts.

By 2004 plans were under way for a new heritage garden just outside the building. A commemorative area for engraved bricks is proving to be a very popular fundraising project. Thanks to volunteers Pat Morrice and Mary Johnson this lasting legacy is a delightful asset to the Cove.

Our dedicated group of volunteers over the years include so many long-time residents without whom the DCHS would not exist. Thank you to Marilyn Myers, Pat Morrice, Vivienne and Arthur Coverdale, Betty Edge, Hazel Best, Jytte Olsen, Rosemary Kenning, Eileen Curtis, Tom Kirk, Audrey Jenkins, Gillian Murray and Carmen Harrington. The list is endless, so please forgive us for not mentioning your name! Eileen Smith, who was brought up in Deep Cove, has taken on the task of cataloguing and scanning photos for our archives and this book. As they say, a photo is worth a thousand words.

The Deep Cove Heritage Garden outside their office in the Deep Cove Cultural Centre. 0942

Today, the DCHS strives to promote understanding and appreciation for the Seymour area and its history. Our organization acquires, preserves and displays the collective memories of our community's history—photographs, documents and transcripts, tapes and videos of interviews with local pioneers. In addition, we are dedicated to educating our community through a variety of outreach programs including presentations to seniors, elementary school students and community groups and visual displays at a variety of accessible public locales (schools, festivals, community days, restaurants, galleries, community centres and other museums). We provide local walking tour pamphlets and guided walking tours and tourist information.

Echoes Across the Inlet was originally published in 1989 and reprinted in 1993 and 2002. This 137-page book tells the history of the Seymour area through stories, anecdotes and photographs and brings the reader up to the 1950s and 60s.

Echoes Across Seymour starts with the story of Mount Seymour, now a provincial park, and continues down to the foot of the mountain and the fjord of Indian Arm Inlet, also now designated as a provincial park. It then goes west to the Seymour River boundary of the Seymour area and continues west across Seymour and its neighbourhoods to Deep Cove. We hope you enjoy a glimpse into where we have come from.

Preface

Echoes Across Seymour attempts to provide the reader with a rare glimpse of the growth of a very special community and is intended as a sequel to *Echoes Across the Inlet,* published by the Deep Cove and Area Heritage Association. The emphasis is on the last fifty years and the changes that have taken place in the area. This volume contains many reminiscences of those residents who played a part in creating the Seymour as we know it today, and also outlines some of the physical challenges in creating a community that wishes to develop in harmony with its beautiful but rugged natural environment.

In 1792 Captain George Vancouver of the Royal Navy, ordered to survey the west coast of North America, met on friendly terms with Spanish explorers Galiano and Valdes in English Bay, just off Spanish Banks. After the meeting, the Spanish continued on to explore Burrard Inlet and its North Arm (now commonly called Indian Arm). A cairn in Cates Park commemorates this event and an old Spanish map of the Indian Arm coastline gives evidence of this early visit. Captain Vancouver carried on north on his original mission to determine whether a reported Northwest Passage really did exist that might be used for British trade to the Orient.

The Royal Navy returned in 1859 to do a detailed survey of Burrard Inlet for defensive purposes. Logging and sawmilling had already commenced in Lynn Valley and Moodyville and would shortly become a major industry in Seymour. The first small neighbourhoods were by this time established to serve the new loggers and mill workers. By 1891 the need for basic municipal services became apparent. The District Municipality of North Vancouver was incorporated by Letters Patent issued in the name of Queen Victoria on August 10, 1891, and encompassed all the accessible lands on the North Shore of Burrard Inlet from Indian Arm to Howe Sound. One of the first major tasks undertaken by the new municipal council was to build a trunk road across the North Shore from the Dollarton waterfront on the east to Eagle Harbour on the west. This was a massive task for a new municipality with few residents.

A.E. McCartney was charged with the responsibility of selecting the best route and building the new road named Keith Road after the second reeve J.O. Keith, whose bank helped finance the project. While the new road provided a sound base for the future, it was quite some time before any significant development took place. It was renamed Mount Seymour Parkway by the province in the 1970s because it served as the main entrance to the province's most visited park.

While British Columbia adopted from Australia a much better system of land registration than was in use in Britain, France, Spain and many states in the USA, the system of granting Crown lands under the Land Act left much to be desired. District lots of hundreds of acres were granted to individuals for relatively small sums of money. After those individuals who were granted land had sold off the timber, many then subdivided the District lots into small residential lots and sold them to the public without roads and services. Eventually most of the small lots came into the possession of the municipality because of the reluctance of residential lot owners to pay taxes on undevelopable land. Most of the early subdivisions were done on a north–south, east–west grid pattern unsuited to development on a mountainside.

The more easily developed central lands, served by Lonsdale Avenue, were incorporated into a new City of North Vancouver in 1907. The westerly part of the District Municipality of North Vancouver was incorporated into the new District Municipality of West Vancouver in 1912. These losses plus the total lack of interest in new development schemes, such as the 1910 upscale Rosslyn proposal in what is now Dollarton, meant that the District of North Vancouver saw little growth until after the Second World War.

In 1948 massive flooding of the Fraser Valley resulted in the government of British Columbia establishing a Lower Mainland Planning Board to create a Lower Mainland Official Regional Plan. The new plan envisaged the future regional community as "a series of cities in a sea of green" with the farmlands protected and most of population growth taken up by the greater Vancouver area. With the later creation of regional districts in British Columbia the four new regional districts of the Lower Mainland were to administer the Lower Mainland Official Regional Plan.

In the mid-1950s both the District and City of North Vancouver were recovering after a long period of provincial receivership brought on by losses associated with damage to Second Narrows Bridge and the Great Depression. In 1955 District council created a Planning and Property Department under the direction of Martin Chesworth, the first municipal planner, Geoff Williams, land agent, and Dave O'Brien, deputy planner. The first goal was to convert the unbuildable grid subdivisions into a new pattern of legal lots and roads that could follow the contours of North Vancouver's steep terrain. Well over one hundred plans were filed under the replotting provisions of the Municipal Act in order to free up land for future development in the District once services became available.

In Seymour the first stages of Windsor Park and Blueridge were built by private developers after the replotting process. In the early 1960s the District made use of the federal Winter Works program to install sewers and upgrade existing roads throughout the municipality. In the mid-1960s a new Land Department was created to organize and manage the District's land assets and to develop and market new municipal subdivisions complete with all services, including underground wiring. Most of the first new neighbourhoods were in the Capilano and Lynn Valley areas to the west but eventually attention turned to "the lands east of Lynn Creek." Until this time the large, sparsely settled eastern area often had been mislabelled as "Deep Cove" or "the Mount Seymour Area," but with the establishment of the District's land development program it was thereafter known as "Seymour."

In the early 1950s the government of Canada encouraged Hooker Chemicals to locate a new chlorine manufacturing plant in the Port of Vancouver to supply the growing BC papermaking industry. The deep-water port could accommodate large ships bringing in salt from Mexico and the BC power grid would easily supply the vast amounts of electricity required by chlorine production. The National Harbours Board (NHB) and the District of North Vancouver would supply the land in Maplewood. Hundreds of acres of ecologically important intertidal lands were lost to industry.

This scene was nearly repeated at the end of the 1960s when the NHB proposed building a large bulk terminal on NHB and District lands, where the Maplewood Conservation Area is presently located. This was also an area recommended by an earlier economic study as a possible site for a Seymour town centre. District Manager Cyril Henderson, about to leave to become Halifax's city manager, recommended to District council that the well-known British planning and development firm Grosvenor International be retained to prepare a plan for the development of Seymour and its future town centre.

The Grosvenor Plan was not well received by the citizens, or by council. It proposed development of 810 ha (2,000 acres) of residential land and 50 ha (122 acres) of town centre, much of that on the Maplewood intertidal mudflats. Out of a proposed population of 65,790, 10,800 people would be living in the town centre. It was projected that by 2004 Seymour would support half of the total population of the District. A citizens' group in Seymour proposed their own plan called the Villages of Seymour, with much more limited development. Council, with awareness of regional population demands, finally asked the District of North Vancouver Planning Department to thoroughly research and prepare a new plan for Seymour with a population limit of 65,000, which was later reduced to 55,000.

In order for the public and council to make fully informed decisions on the plan, a series of eleven research reports were published by the planning department on such areas of interest as protecting the natural environment, transportation, housing options and regional goals. The Seymour Official Community Plan (OCP) was adopted in 1985. Concepts developed in the Seymour OCP for a wide range of needed housing and environmental protection were later included in the District OCP of 1990. The Seymour OCP has since been abandoned and the Seymour Local Plan adopted proposing very limited housing growth.

CHAPTER 1

Mount Seymour Alpine Area

Millions of visitors and armchair travellers around the world picture Vancouver with a beautiful mountain backdrop towering above a magnificent deep-sea harbour. The District of North Vancouver, incorporated in 1891, has always been a very special, almost magnetic, draw for outdoor adventurers. The challenges of the upper ski slopes and trails of Mount Seymour and the Fannin Range to the north are irresistible. Mount Seymour in recent years has experienced a tremendous growth in both winter sports and year-round trail use. Along with this growth came a rising number of dramatic rescues and the occasional tragedy.

Mount Seymour and surrounding communities, September 2009. Photo by Vickie Boughen, 3419

Top: Ski time on Mount Seymour, 1953.

Above: Mystery Lake at Mount Seymour, 1952.

Illustrations by Adrien Germiquet, courtesy Wendy Rasmussen, 1554, 1552

The Alpine Area comprises 100 sq km (25,000 acres) and covers approximately two-thirds of the District of North Vancouver developments on the North Shore. Traditionally these developments were kept mainly to the lower slopes to reflect a certain harmony with nature. The area has often been threatened by development proposals that would seriously impact the natural environment. These proposals included plans for exploration of highway routes through both the Capilano and Seymour valleys and along the west side of Indian Arm; a major gas pipeline to the north through the Alpine Area; an attempt to build a mining road through the headwaters of Lynn Creek to open up early mining claims; a residential neighbourhood and a hotel on top of Grouse Mountain; a resort on Kennedy Lake accessible only by helicopter; and the logging of the two regional watersheds and of provincial lands on Indian Arm.

The most shocking proposal came in 1983 with the threat to log forestlands on the south face of Grouse Mountain. North Vancouver council took immediate action to implement new protective measures for the Alpine areas. Upon the recommendation of municipal planner Kai Kreuchen, council instructed the Planning Department to conduct a detailed study of the Alpine Area with the view of creating an Official Community Plan (OCP) that would guide and regulate any future development. The North Vancouver District's portion of Indian Arm, due to its close relationship with the mountains, was to be included in the community planning process.

The sixty-three-page *Alpine Area Background Report* published in September 1984 outlined natural resources and land uses. The well-received report contained valuable feedback from local residents that was later included in the planning process. Council adopted the Alpine Area OCP in July 1986. The *North Shore News* reported that the Canadian Institute of Planners had presented its highest award for planning excellence in Canada to the District of North Vancouver for the Alpine Area OCP.

CHRONOLOGY—MOUNT SEYMOUR

1864–69 Frederick Seymour is the governor of the British Colony of British Columbia

1908 BC Mountaineering Club records first climb of Mount Seymour

1929 Alpine Club of Canada applies for a 274-ha (677-acre) lease and runs the area for several years (the Depression years forced the club to drop its lease)

1936 Mount Seymour Provincial Park established with a total of 274 ha (677 acres)

Harold Enquist purchases 121 ha (300 acres) from the provincial government at $25 per acre to develop a ski area and rustic accommodation facilities

1938 BC Forestry Service surveys and builds the first road to take skiers halfway up the mountain to the Mushroom parking lot (6 km/3.75 mi) and the trail to Enquist Ski Camp

1941 Tommy Hunter designs and builds first ski jump on current half-pipe site

1949 Provincial government purchases Harold Enquist's operation and hires him to run it. First lift, Sun Bowl rope tow, installed

1950 Access road extended to what is currently P2 road continues to the base area

1951 Harold Enquist's park-use permit expires. The Forest Service advertises for local concessionaires to run the lifts, ski school and cafeteria

1953 CBC constructs the first high-elevation broadcasting site in Canada on Mount Seymour. It began broadcasting on December 13. These towers transmitted television for the first time to western Canada and are a Vancouver landmark visible from all over the Lower Mainland

1950s–70s Provincial government expands the park to the present size of approximately 3,650 ha (9,000 acres). Lifts and runs are developed. Different concessionaires run the assorted departments

1984 The Wood family purchases the area under the name of Mount Seymour Resorts Limited

Lodge and Brockton chairlifts are added

1984–2004 Western Canada's largest rental shop constructed

First Snow Tube park and first in-ground half-pipe on the West Coast built

1998 First Nations claim the land

Environmental History

Through the ages, Seymour's mountain backdrop has had a major effect on its local climate. Moisture-laden winds coming in from the Pacific Ocean are forced to rise up as they pass over Mount Seymour, cool, and then deposit heavy rain and snow on the mountain. Presently the snow melts away during spring and summer. However, thousands of years ago during a period of global cooling the snow of the Coast Mountains did not melt but compacted into glacial ice, eventually creating a huge ice sheet, aptly named the Seymour Ice Sheet, 2,300 m (about 7,600 ft) thick. The Seymour Ice Sheet and two more that followed pushed the Seymour landscape downward and moved slowly southward grinding down the mountaintops, scouring out the valleys and finally depositing vast amounts of glacial till on the lower slopes.

Upon the warming of the planet the great ice sheets began to melt and plant life began anew. First it was the lichens and mosses, then the ground-cover plants, deciduous trees, mixed forests, and finally the giant conifers, cedars and Douglas firs. With the renewal of their habitat, the birds and wildlife soon returned. The salmon arrived in great numbers in the new streams that had been created by the glacial runoff. Into this "Eden of Nature" came the aboriginal peoples, the First Nations, to establish their settlements long before the arrival of the first European explorers.

There are several mountain peaks within the park boundary apart from Mount Seymour, including Mount Bishop and Mount Elsay. Seymour itself is made up of three peaks called First Pump, Second Pump and Third Pump. Mount Bishop has the highest elevation at 1,509 m (4,951 ft) and then Mount Seymour, 1,449 m (4,754 ft) high.

Mount Seymour was named after Frederick Seymour, who was the second governor of BC, from 1864 to 1869. There are two other mountains named after Governor Seymour in BC: Mount Seymour on Quadra Island in the Strait of Georgia and Mount Seymour on Moresby Island on Haida Gwaii (Queen Charlotte Islands). Seymour Street, familiar to most Vancouverites, was also named for him.[1]

Lakes in the park include Flower Lake, Goldie Lake and Elsay Lake (which is the largest). All of these drain eastward into

Gwynn Jenkins on Mount Seymour, 1952. Photo by Audrey Jenkins, 3261

Indian Arm. Lakes that are further westward (First and Second lakes and Hidden Lake) drain into the Seymour River to the west.

Tsleil-Waututh: First Peoples on the Mountain

Mount Seymour was the traditional hunting grounds for the Tsleil-Waututh First Nation people. They hunted game, including elk, and collected berries. Yellow cedar bark was used for clothing, ropes, baskets, hats, blankets and cradles. The tree rings are important to many First Nations people because they believe they represent the presence of their ancestors and the connection to the land.

"Mountain Path"
from *Salish Poems* by Wil to Write (Wil George)

Mountain there is a path
through the bramble and
brush
around the rock and stone
jagged sharp edges
I find a path here
winding around the mountain.
My elders counsel,
"use caution when you walk
the mountain path in the dark"
Mountain there is a path
in rain and fog I move
caution stepping with some
difficulty
still I continue along
my mountain path

Industry

Early logging of the mountain started in the 1880s. The Hastings Mill Company logged the west side of the mountain for cedar and fir in the 1920s. The east side was logged by Buck Logging Company (see *Echoes Across the Inlet* for more early logging history). Today logging operations no longer exist but there is still some evidence of Buck's Logging trails and skid roads. The trees that stand are second growth.[2]

Postcard of Mount Seymour Lodge, ca. 1961. Photo by George Weinhaupl, courtesy Vickie Boughen, 0996

Recreation

During the 1930s people started to build cabins on Mount Seymour—at one point there were about 200 on the mountain. When the Alpine Club cabin was officially opened in September 1931, more than thirty members of the club celebrated with a meal of venison. A stay in the cabin cost ten cents a day per person during the week or twenty-five cents on weekends.[3]

Hikers would make the 6.5-km (4-mi) climb to reach the cabins using "bug lights" (candles carried in tin cans) in the dark—some bug lights were kept in trees for communal use and borrowed using an honour system. It must have been a magical sight to see the lights coming through the forest to the cabins. There was a real cabin community on the mountain and

Cabin on First Lake, ca. 1938. Courtesy Donna Leighton, 1880

folks would get together for dinners and dances. Pressure from this community is what drove the government to create the provincial park in 1936.

The government wanted to avoid having cabins built all over the mountain so they granted land leases for private cabin construction. Today the owners of the remaining cabins pay a lease of $575 per year.

Local resident Eileen Smith recalls fond memories from the 1960s of the UBC Varsity Outdoor Club cabin with its two big dorms, bunks stacked three high and a big room with floor-to-ceiling fireplace where students and members gathered with guitars to sing popular folk songs.

The Forest Services Rangers cabin was built by Ole Johansen in the 1940s with 15-cm (6-in) diameter yellow cedar logs. Ole lived there with his family. Their water was provided from a stream behind the cabin. The cabin was improved over the years and eventually grew to 250 sq m (2,700 sq ft) over two floors. It was later occupied by BC Parks staff.

By the 1980s the logs were rotting and the cabin faced demolition but Earl Pletch took over the repair work and tinned the roof. In 1994 resort general manager Eddie Wood and his family moved in, followed in 2000 by Alex Douglas, his wife, and dog Seymour. With help from Brent Watson renovations continue to this day. Alex tells the tale that Ole said the stone fireplace was built "in two days with two cases of beer." Those were the days.

Summer

Mount Seymour offers visitors a variety of activities during the summer months. There are fourteen hiking trails that range in difficulty and length and a variety of

Top left: Hirschberg family picnicking on Mount Seymour. Courtesy Donna Leighton, 2395

Above right: Stirrat family at lake on Mount Seymour. Courtesy Robert Stirrat, 0587

Left: Baring-It-All Gang on Mount Seymour, ca. 1939. Courtesy Donna Leighton, 1872

designated mountain biking trails. Fishing, picnicking, camping and wildlife viewing are also available. The mountain provides visitors with many spectacular viewpoints of Vancouver and Indian Arm Provincial Park.

Deep Cove's very own Charles (Chaz) Romalis is probably one of Canada's original mountain bike enthusiasts. The self-made millionaire and owner of Deep Cove Bikes has spent more than twenty years promoting the sport.

Chaz grew up with Mount Seymour in his backyard and now all the North Shore Mountains and Whistler attract riders from around the world. Global TV documented his climb to fame in a 2004 film called *Bumpy History*.

Winter

Mount Seymour has long been a popular winter destination for locals and visitors alike. The mountain provides a variety of terrain to suit beginners and more advanced skiers and snowboarders. With the longest-running professional ski and snowboard school on the North Shore, the mountain now boasts three progressive terrain parks for snowboard enthusiasts. Many amateur and professional ski and snowboard athletes from the Seymour Team have been involved in national and international competitions and events.

Mount Seymour has more than ten kilometres (6.25 miles) of alpine and forest trails that are marked and maintained for snowshoeing. These dedicated snowshoe trails can be explored as part of a guided interpretive tour or on one's own.

Snow tubing and tobogganing are also available at the Enquist Tube Park.

Ole Johansen's cabin on Mount Seymour. Courtesy Terry Tobin, 1701

Top left: Alex Douglas. Photo by John Pavlik, 4523

Top right: Twin Tow, Mount Seymour rope tow. Courtesy Terry Tobin, 1698

Above: Ian Beaton and friends skiing on Mount Seymour. Courtesy Debbie Smith, 0776

People

Alex Douglas: The Mount Seymour History Project's (MSHP) mission is to preserve the written and physical history of Mount Seymour. Founder Alex Douglas works to share that history through displays, special events, multimedia and education programs for the North Shore community and the Greater Vancouver area.

This history includes that of the early hikers, the first cabins in the Greater Vancouver Regional District lands including the early Enquist Ski Camp and cabins within the provincial park, and the logging of Mount Seymour. Alex has a particular interest in all of the different ski clubs that have used Mount Seymour over the years including the Mount Seymour Ski Club, Tyrol Club and the Westminster Ski Runners Club. In 1997 the general manager of Mount Seymour Resorts Limited, Eddie Wood, allowed Alex to use the Mount Seymour Ski Club room in the "Lowers" to set up a temporary meeting room and museum. The building is actually the old UBC Varsity Outdoor Club cabin. Alex has recorded stories of ski pioneers Ole Johansen, Blanche Middleton and Harold Enquist and many others. He welcomes new stories and photos and is working on a permanent home for his wonderful collection of old ski and mountain equipment (see *Echoes Across the Inlet* chapter 10 for early days of skiing on the mountain).[4]

Above: Ski jumper Milt "Mac" McLachlan, ca. 1938. Courtesy Donna Leighton, 1887

Right: Wilf Veysey in competition, 1932–33. Courtesy Valerie Remedios, 1563

Kevin Sansalone: Mount Seymour has been the home of snowboarding since the beginning of the sport. Kevin was an original member of the "Seymour Kids" crew famous for its pioneering spirit in the sport. He has won a gold medal at Winter X-Games and is involved with competing, filming and marketing, snowboard construction and design.

Devun Walsh: Another Seymour Kid success story. He currently runs Wildcats, a snowboarding production company, and he has appeared in many snowboard movies.

Olympic Connections

With Mount Seymour known as a training ground and the affordable mountain for locals it is not surprising that it has produced its fair share of Olympic-calibre downhill skiers, snowboarders and cross-country skiers.

Ross Rebagliati: This Canadian Olympic gold medal winner in snowboarding at the 1998 Olympic Winter Games remembers that Seymour was the first mountain where he and his family went downhill skiing in the early 1980s. They went up with the cross-country skis they had used in Saskatchewan, not realizing that the West Coast kids had slightly different equipment. Ross jumped and telemarked down the hill. For their next trip, they rented more appropriate equipment.

Ross recalls asking for size seven based on his shoe size. "The guy laughed and said, 'You probably could use some one-twenties.' It sounded long until I saw them."

He started ski racing and seven years later started racing snowboards. Ross's book *Off the Chain* describes his journey

Left: Manny Osborne-Paradis. Courtesy Jane E. Osborne, 4633

Below: Couple with sled, February 1939. Courtesy Donna Leighton, 1876

through the rise of snowboarding from its fringe beginnings to the multimillion-dollar industry it has become.

Manuel Osborne-Paradis: Growing up in Deep Cove, he has been described by his mother, Jane Osborne, as "a kid born with an illegal amount of energy." She realized early on that an outlet was needed for her fuel-injected son, so she and her father, Dr. Jim Osborne, introduced Manny to alpine skiing at the age of three. He took readily to the slopes. He remembers, "I didn't really like to ski, I just liked to jump—that was my big thing."

At age fifteen he moved to Invermere, BC, to join the provincial ski team. At the 2010 Olympics in Vancouver he pursued his goal "to be the fastest downhill skier in the world."

Above: Black bear. Photo by Damon Calderwood, 3275

Below: Black-tailed deer. Photo by Damon Calderwood, 3276

Environment

Al Grass, well-known park naturalist and member of the Vancouver Natural History Society, describes Mount Seymour Provincial Park as home to a wide variety of birds such as hawks, falcons, geese, owls, woodpeckers, tanagers and various types of crossbills.

Many small mammals inhabit the area including shrews, voles, chipmunks, Douglas and northern flying squirrels and hares. Larger mammals can be found living on the mountain, including coyotes, American black bears, mountain lions, bobcats, mountain goats and deer.[5]

Black bears come closer to the nearby residential area each year and many locals have reported bear visitors in their backyards. See the Blueridge chapter for more details.

The Elders Council for Parks in British Columbia: The council is described as "an independent society of mostly retired people, from the national, provincial and regional parks agencies and conservation advocates, with a passion for parks," by Mel Turner, retired BC Parks planning and management executive. The Elders Council established a five-year agreement with BC Parks to use the Mount Seymour Provincial Park Ranger Station, located at the entrance to the park, as a Heritage Centre. The centre will house a history of BC Parks and offer programs to participants of all ages who will have an opportunity to enjoy nature through guided "Talks and Walks." The special Teddy Bear Picnics series teaches bear awareness and the importance of parks to the very young.

Last year, 2011, marked one hundred years of recreation and protection in BC that began with the preservation of Strathcona Provincial Park on Vancouver Island.

CHAPTER 2

Indian Arm

Today, the official name of Indian Arm Inlet is Say Nuth Khaw Yum Heritage Park/Indian Arm Provincial Park. Say Nuth Khaw Yum translates literally to "Serpent's Land." This area is at the heart of the traditional territory of the Tsleil-Waututh people (see chapter 9). Indian Arm Inlet has been continuously utilized by the Tsleil-Waututh First Nation, the "People of the Inlet," as a hunting and fishing ground since time out of mind and remains today an area of great cultural significance.

In 2012 Say Nuth Khaw Yum Heritage Park/Indian Arm Provincial Park includes 6,826 ha (17,000 acres) along the eastern

West shore of Indian Arm, 1953. Courtesy District of North Vancouver, 2732

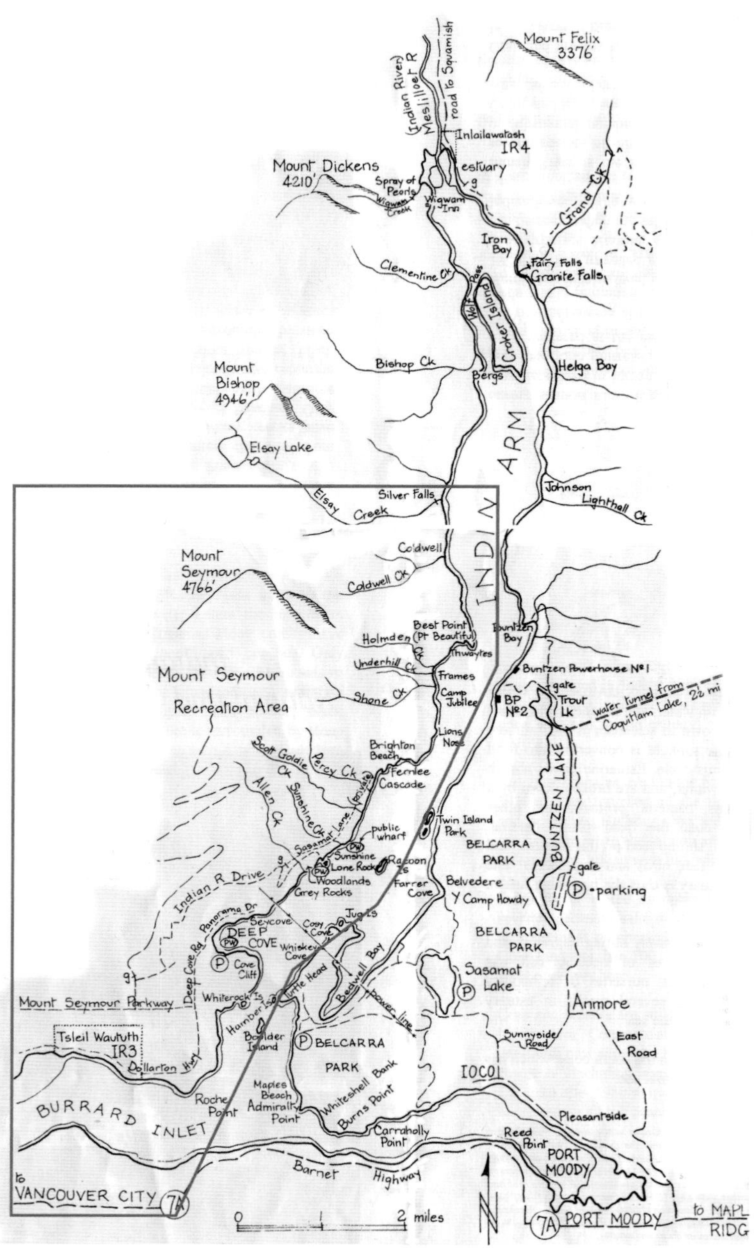

Above: Indian Arm illustration by Liz Shelton, from the Indian Arm Natural and Cultural History brochure. 4127

Top right: View up Indian Arm: the tip of Belcarra, Racoon Island and Twin Islands. Photo by Vickie Boughen, 3426

and western shorelines of the upper portion of Indian Arm. The park is co-managed by the Tsleil-Waututh First Nation, BC Parks and Port Metro Vancouver. The co-management scheme attempts to provide park visitors with a unique contemporary experience of Tsleil-Waututh and Coast Salish culture and history.[6]

Indian Arm is a mysteriously beautiful fjord, yet this north arm of Burrard Inlet lies half forgotten despite the fact it is within an hour's journey of the homes of 2.3 million people. Probably over the years more tourists than residents have seen its rugged shores from the decks of a long succession of tour boats that have plied its waters. For most residents Indian Arm is Deep Cove: Panorama Beach, the government wharf, the cafés, the visitors and more. For a few boating enthusiasts Indian Arm represents launching a boat at Cates Park for a quick spin around Twin Islands then over to Sunshine Falls and back, or perhaps an afternoon's water-skiing off Belcarra. Not too many people have enjoyed the experience of an evening cruise through the upper fjord with the outlines of the incredibly steep forested slopes seen through the mists layered one upon the other, plunging down into the depths of the sea. Even fewer have ventured below the surface to experience the exhilaration of exploring the undersea life around Croker or Racoon islands. Perhaps the most privileged of all are those who can enjoy Indian Arm at any time from their own homes on its shores.

With privilege and land use come responsibilities. The private sector that has access to the Arm must "tread lightly" and leave it in as good a state as they found it. The public sector must ensure public safety

Left: Indian Arm estuary and Wigwam Inn, 1953. Courtesy District of North Vancouver, 2804

Below: Postcard of the north arm of Burrard Inlet, 1934. Courtesy Robert Stirrat, 0603

while protecting and preserving the natural amenities for today and tomorrow. Many levels of public administration are concerned with the future of Indian Arm. Some of the concerns cross the boundaries of municipal jurisdiction and involve regional, provincial and even federal authority. Because of this we should take a broad look at Indian Arm with particular emphasis on lands, waters and facilities located within municipal boundaries. With a third of the shoreline and the two major access points, Deep Cove and Cates

CHRONOLOGY—INDIAN ARM PROVINCIAL PARK

1905 Twin Island established as an early provincial recreational reserve

1951 Racoon Island established as recreational reserve

1981 Twin and Racoon island reserves officially elevated to Provincial Park status

1995 Indian Arm Provincial Park established as part of the Lower Mainland Nature Legacy initiative

1998 Say Nuth Khaw Yum/Indian Arm Provincial Park officially established. A collaborative management agreement is signed between the Tsleil-Waututh and BC Parks, creating a Park Management Board designed to oversee park management, conservation, recreation and cultural heritage objectives

Park, located within the District of North Vancouver (DNV), the municipality does have a very special interest in the future of Indian Arm.

Looking north at the end of the inlet past Wigwam Inn, 2010. 3551

The slopes on either side of Indian Arm are spectacular, with typical slopes in the Sunshine to Cascade area approaching 40 percent. Slopes as steep as 70 percent can be found a short distance in from the western shore. Only a few areas on the Arm north of Woodlands have enough gently sloping land to offer development possibilities. In the District these are the areas between Brighton Beach and Frames Landing at about 20 percent and to a lesser extent the area immediately north of Silver Falls, at about 30 percent.

Further up the inlet, Bergs, Clementine and Wigwam on the western shore offer the most level ground together with minor areas on the eastern shore, south of Granite Falls, and the Village of Belcarra.

In 2010 the Say Nuth Khaw Yum/Indian Arm Provincial Park Plan, developed by the Tsleil-Waututh in collaboration with BC Parks and Port Metro Vancouver, was officially approved. The plan includes a bioregional atlas, land use designations including Tsleil-Waututh management areas and recommendations for marine area designations. Leah George-Wilson, director of the Tsleil-Waututh Treaty, Lands and Resources Department, said the plan "is the culmination of over a decade of effort and is an important example of what can be achieved through collaboration. Our experience has shown us that great things can happen when we work together toward a common goal." Ernest (Ernie) George, Tsleil-Waututh elder and park management board member, added: "The preparation of this plan has been a long journey...a journey not just about forging a new approach to protected areas management, but also a journey of reconciliation and cooperation."[7]

The Tsleil-Waututh Legend of Scnoki

—as told by Annie George, 1966

After the flood, as the waters receded from the earth, they left behind a gigantic reptile, known to the Indians as Scnoki.

The terrible monster had heads at both ends. It was fastened to the rocks and suspended like a huge one-span bridge over Lions Nose, the narrowest part of Burrard Inlet, known as Kapulpaqua.

All living things that approached it would curl, twist up and die instantly. For generations, people portaged their canoes over the hill, rather than risking death by crossing the great serpent's body.

The hearts of the people were cold with fear and they longed for deliverance from the accursed thing. None dared to approach it, much less attack it, lest some vengeance should be wrought upon them.

Eventually a man who had once been captured by the Scnoki returned to kill the dreaded monster. One after another spears found their mark and as the eighth went straight to the target, Scnoki relaxed his hold on the rocks, slowly drew his colossal body across the inlet, climbed over the mountains, disappeared into Lake Buntzen and was seen no more.

For those who doubt the truth of this story, the First Nations people will show them the rocks on either side of the inlet that still bear the marks where Scnoki's awful heads were fastened. It is said that on the ground over which his frightful body crawled, no living thing has ever grown. No blade of grass and no moss thrive there to this day.

According to an account by Whitney Spearing, the waters of Indian Arm may actually harbour a real sea serpent, what scientists call a "marine cryptic." As recently as 2000, residents of Seymour have identified what researchers claim to be a *Cadborosaurus willsi*, or "Caddy" for short, swimming in the waters off properties on Lowry Lane and Beachview Drive. The creature was spotted attacking and eating whole waterfowl.

Apparently there is only one set of photos that documents the Cadborosaurus in its entirety. These photos were taken at Naden Harbour whaling station in 1937, when a Caddy carcass was discovered inside the stomach of a recently harvested whale. The photos show the creature's ten-foot long serpentine body, small front flippers and a camel-like head.

Environment

Indian Arm is officially known as the North Arm of Burrard Inlet and extends some 20 km (12.7 mi) in a north-north-easterly

Tsleil-Waututh graphic of the sea serpent Scnoki. Courtesy Tsleil-Waututh Nation, 4477

direction from the main harbour. It ranges from 1 km (0.6 mi) wide just north of Best Point to 4.5 km (2.8 mi) wide between Deep Cove and Farrer Cove. It is one of the deepest arms of the sea on the coast hereabouts with a depth of 220 m (720 ft) recorded near Best Point. This compares to a maximum depth of 62 m (204 ft) in the main harbour. An underwater shelf across the mouth of the arm between Roche Point (Cates Park) and Admiralty Point (Belcarra Regional Park) at a depth of 26 m (85 ft) forms a deep-water dam that prevents full circulation of the lower levels of water. As a result the normal flushing action expected of a river-fed tidal inlet is inhibited; thus, only the top 20 m (65.5 ft) of water receives adequate oxygenation to support subsurface life.

Much of Indian Arm is uninhabited land that supports a large variety of wildlife. Common mammalian species include black bear, blacktail deer, cougar, coyote and red fox. Over seventy species of birds have been identified within the provincial park area, some of which are overwintering waterfowl. Harbour seals, five species of salmon, sea-run cutthroat, steelhead, rockfish, anemones, nudibranches, tritons, shrimp, clams and mussels are among the marine species inhabiting these waters. Crabs and other shellfish are extremely plentiful and use the area off Twin Islands as a breeding ground. The estuary at the top of Indian Arm is a vital habitat for both prawns and crabs. An especially spectacular event in Indian Arm is the biannual pink salmon run that begins in July and runs into October.[8]

Top right: Red squirrel. Photo by Damon Calderwood, 3281

Below: Red fox. Photo by Damon Calderwood, 3280

Recreation

For the experienced paddler Indian Arm offers extraordinary canoeing and kayaking. All paddlers require a tide chart in order to identify optimal times for travelling up or down the Arm. Northbound watercraft headed for the top of Indian Arm should travel on a rising tide and vice versa. Paddling up the Arm takes roughly two hours while moving with the current. The Indian Arm Estuary can be navigated upstream for 1 km (.62 mi) at high tide and offers unique wildlife viewing opportunities.

Wigwam Inn is currently an outpost station for the Royal Vancouver Yacht

Left: Sudden weather changes are prevalent in the inlet. Photo courtesy The Province, 4640

Below: 4528

Bottom: Kayaking in Indian Arm is a popular activity, 2011. 4769

Club. However, the location of Wigwam does not fall under the DNV jurisdiction, and therefore will not be covered in this book. Please refer to *Echoes Across the Inlet* and the Deep Cove Heritage Society archives for more detailed information on the early history of this iconic heritage building.

Communities

The foreshore on the west side of the Arm from Deep Cove in the south to Best Point, and from Silver Falls to the Indian River in the north is privately held. Much of the foreshore from Deep Cove to Best Point is increasingly being used for permanent residences or summer cottages.

Gray Rocks: This area continues to be boat-access only, making development challenging. Currently, some owners are asking the DNV to allow upgrading of a hydro services road to allow better access to their properties.[9]

Above: Woodlands community, 1953. Courtesy District of North Vancouver, 2806

Below: Brighton Beach, 2010. 3586

Woodlands: Many people think that Deep Cove was the first neighbourhood to be settled in the Indian Arm area, but Woodlands, located just north of Deep Cove, attracted people to settle there by the early 1900s. Woodlands gained a reputation as a choice summer resort for many prominent Vancouver residents. The first permanent residents were the Hugh Myddleton Wood family. The first annual community Woodlands Regatta was held in 1910, and the regatta continues to this day. Woodlands was accessible only by water until 1917. Road construction began soon after, but it was many more years before the road was completed.[10] Today Woodlands is the home of mainly permanent residents and in many respects has retained its charm with no major changes. A more detailed history of the Woodlands area is covered in *Echoes Across the Inlet*, chapter 4.

Lone Rock (Teepoorten Island): Lone Rock was purchased by Julius Teepoorten in 1912. He transformed the barren rock into a beautiful garden and summer home for his family of eight children. He named the island Samarkand, meaning "heart's desire." The family had to sell the island after the stock market crash of 1929.[11]

Cascade: Cascade was the original site of a rock quarry. Today, there are year-round residents with a private road called Sasamat Lane. There is currently no water service to this area.[12]

Brighton Beach: In 1886 pioneer John Rainey moved here and pre-empted 100 ha (245 acres) of land that encompassed both Brighton Beach and Camp Jubilee areas. Rainey developed gardens and orchards on the property, and attempted to mine for gold and silver.[13] Rainey passed away in 1913, and the property was left alone until 1939, when it was purchased by a group of First World War veterans who formed the Army and Navy Veterans Association (ANVA). Since then most of the veterans have sold their properties.[14]

Camp Jubilee: John Joseph Banfield established his summer home up Indian Arm in 1913 at Orlomah Beach, which his granddaughter Jane Banfield explains he named after his three children and wife; ORson, LOis, MAy and Harriet. The Banfield family spent $10,000—an enormous sum at that time—clearing and cultivating gardens on the property. In 1934 John Banfield passed away, and his family sold the property. Shortly thereafter the women of the Workers Unity League founded Camp Jubilee Retreat on the property. Initially the retreat was aimed towards children from working-class families who were on social welfare. Volunteers gave huge amounts of time and energy to raise funds for the camp until the 1970s, when it closed. Camp Jubilee remained closed throughout the 1980s, but is now open again. Indian Arm Recreational Services operates summer camps, retreats and conferences from the Camp Jubilee and Conference Centre.[15]

Lions Nose: Lions Nose is named after the distinctive rock formation along the cliffs. This is one of several pictograph sites in the inlet where First Nations people have recorded their dreams and visions. The rule is: observe these rock paintings from the water only and do not touch.[16]

Frames Landing: In 1910 Statira Frame bought a lot and the area was named Frames Landing. There, she built the cottage that was to become her summer home.[17] She was a friend of the famous artist Emily Carr, who visited the cottage at least once. Two of Frame's paintings are in the permanent collection of the Vancouver Art Gallery.

Thwaytes Landing: Captain Thwaytes and his wife came to the inlet in 1927. They built the original house and operated a chicken farm on the 53-ha (130-acre) property. Mearnie Summers bought the land from Thwaytes in 1970 and lived there until 1996.[18]

Camp Jubilee, 2010. 3581

Best Point aka Point Beautiful: Best Point was the site of "a house of ill repute" at the turn of the century, during construction of the power plant across the

Thwaytes Landing area, 2010. 3572

Top and above: Sunshine Regatta, 1963. Courtesy Tom Kirk, 1268, 1264

Right: Looking south to Best Point, 2010. 3570

inlet at Buntzen.[19] Tales were told that in the 1930s the workers from the Buntzen Power House came across to Best Point where they were entertained by "ladies of the night."[20]

Coldwell Beach: Local summer resident Bob Garries says that Coldwell Beach was named after one of the original aldermen of the City of Vancouver. The Allardice/Eaton clan bought 11 ha (27 acres) at Coldwell Beach in 1958. Two old cabins on each side of the creek provided space for three families, with about thirteen children among them. Mothers and children lived in the cabins from July 1 to September 1, while fathers commuted back and forth to jobs in Vancouver.

Don and Ethel Allardice hosted a Mount Seymour Lions summer party at the property every year during the 1970s. Rock cod was buried in a pit with coals and served with Ethel's famous black bean sauce. Mussels by the sack full were collected, steamed and devoured.

Today two families, the Sperlings and the Johnsons, live there year round. The Allardice, Garries and Eaton families still own property.

Silver Falls: The land at Silver Falls is privately owned. The area is of great cultural importance to the Tsleil-Waututh Nation. Elders remember their parents warning them not to look at the falls because it was a place of bad omens. Looking could cause blindness or bring bad luck.[21] Today members of the Tsleil-Waututh Nation continue to respect the power of the falls and warn travellers to follow the words of their ancestors. Obviously no photo attached!

People

Captain Thwaytes: Times were tough in 1961, as shown in an exchange of letters between poultry-farm owner Captain Thwaytes and shop owner of Woodlands Water Grocery, Wilfred Laubach. Thwaytes writes: "I seem to be losing out on the Woodlands market, in spite of the weather. I have only sold half the number of eggs to you that I sold last year. If necessary, I intend to peddle them over from here to Dollarton at 50 cents a dozen in cartons. I am operating in the red."

Laubach replies: "You are getting all the egg business from Woodlands that is available. I have some serious problems about my own business as you know. The chain stores are competing so strenuously against each other these days eggs are one of their competitive items selling at times at two dozen for 89 cents! The price of coke and orange are still the same, $1.20 per dozen."

Today some things have not changed, as big box stores and supermarkets strenuously attempt to put the small retailer out of business.

Mearnie Summers: Mearnie Summers, one of the modern pioneers of the inlet from 1970–96, was the saviour of many greenhorn residents. She purchased Captain Thwaytes' property at Thwaytes Landing in 1970 and set out to do major renovations to the house. Leaded windows, a copper-faced fireplace and many improvements made it into a cozy comfortable home. Mearnie was a physical education teacher, a dance teacher at Vancouver's two universities and an accomplished sailor. For many years Mearnie tackled everything from constructing septic fields and wharves to building cottages, and lent a willing, helping hand to residents in trouble. She also had her own barge that she used to help transport furniture and household items. Living up the Arm brought many challenges. Mearnie and her long-time companion, Jean, narrowly escaped being buried by a debris torrent from Holmden Creek in 1990.

Left: Don Allardice and a Japanese guest serving rock cod. Courtesy Suzanne Allardice, 2512

Below left: Mearnie Summers. Courtesy Caffyn Kelley, 4586

Below: Diving in at Coldwell Beach. Courtesy Suzanne Allardice, 2511

Excerpt from "I Don't Know Them"

—by Meg Troy

Looking up Indian Arm I see nothing but low lying clouds

Ghostly shapes of peoples past that hover silently over the Deep Cove water

As hard as I squint my eyes, I don't know them

Unrecognizable souls, swooping down to kiss this lonely fool

Sitting afloat on such a foreboding day . . . impatiently waiting for the sun to shine

My mind is drifting back to when fish were plentiful

When families on these shorelines knew each other's names and celebrated their diversity

Below left: Madge Winfield steering her seaborne supermarket, 1954. Photo by Jack Long, Weekend Magazine, *4529*

Below right: The Sea Biscuit. *Courtesy Bev and Doug Shaw, 0432*

Transportation and Services

Many changes have taken place over the years for residents of the inlet. Fifty years ago regular visits up and down the Arm were made by the Harbour Navigation vessel *Scenic.* This valiant boat braved the wind, rain and fog to deliver groceries, mail, parcels and plenty of local gossip. It was a lifeline to the people who had chosen to live in Vancouver's wilderness.

Woodlands Water Grocery: Woodlands Water Grocery began operation in 1936 under the ownership of Jessie and Percy Squire. Jessie acted as the unofficial postmistress for twenty-nine years.

By 1946 Woodlands Water Grocery store was in full swing. The following year Marjorie (Madge) Winfield partnered with Margaret and Jim Masson and for six years Madge brightened up the lives of North Arm shoppers with her "sailing supermarket," formerly known as the *Sea Biscuit.* Her personalized service for her "folks" included buying just the right shade of new lipstick, cashing cheques, getting prescriptions refilled, matching crochet cotton, taking films to be developed, buying customers' favourite magazines and much more.

In 1974 the last owner, Wilfred Lauback, closed the store.

BC Floating Post Office: The floating post office is known worldwide to stamp collectors as the Burrard Inlet TPO (Travelling Post Office). Captain Stalker used to receive many requests from collectors asking him to stamp their letters with the TPO stamp.

CHRONOLOGY—BURRARD INLET TRAVELLING POST OFFICE

1908 On January 1 the Burrard Inlet floating post office begins service. At one time it was the only floating post office in the Commonwealth and was operated under the name New Brighton Ferry Company.[22]

1913 Harbour Shipping Company opens and begins to service Burrard Inlet and Indian Arm

1914 John "Andy" Anderson begins to work at Harbour Shipping Company and operates the post office for many years

1920 Captain J. Douglas Stalker buys Harbour Shipping Company[23]

1930 MV *Scenic* is purchased by Captain Stalker and added to the company's ship fleet[24]

1950s Captain Stalker sells his interest in the company[25]

1960 Captain Stalker retires from operating the MV *Scenic* when he is well over eighty years[26] old. Captain Bob Brace takes over from him

Skipper Joe Blackmun delivered mail on the *Wee Willie*, 6-metre (20-foot) Harbour Ferries craft. October 30, 1970, was the final day of sixty-two years of mail service by boat.[27]

Water Taxi: Art George started a water taxi in the early 1940s. Art knew every nook and cranny of the North Arm and regularly ferried people up the inlet from his marina. For details on Art's influence on the area see *Echoes Across the Inlet*, page 112.

B. Kenna with the Deep Cove Water Taxi, 1952. Courtesy Art George, 0281

By 1971 Jimmy (Jeep) Pattison took over the business and for the following twenty years serviced the locals with water taxi service. Until 1992 he ferried the children living on the inlet to and from their homes to school in Deep Cove. After funding from the school board ceased he could no longer afford to operate the service.

Today West Coast Power Boat Handling owned by Jimmy Watt operates a Deep Cove Water Taxi on a charter basis. He has plied the waters of the inlet for over thirty years and is well known for his volunteer work on the Deep Cove Search and Rescue lifeboat.

The 2010 census showed approximately thirty permanent-resident families who have to rely on their own resources for year-round survival. Although modern communication and technology keeps them in touch with the world, they do have to provide their own water transportation if they are located beyond the end of the road access at Sunshine. See the 2009 Indian Arm District of North Vancouver Report for details.

Excerpt from "The Indian River Road"

—*From* Songs of Indian Arm: A Tribute in Poetry *by John Stevenson*

The 1957 Chevrolet
shudders and rattles
on the washboard road
under drenched trees
water pours
down the mountain
fills the ditches
The rough road
twists on through
sodden wilderness
The hairpin turns
hurry down
in leaps
and dips
to the swollen wharf
by the wrinkled sea.

North Shore Rescue, Auxiliary II. Photo by Robin Biggin, North Shore Rescue, 4446

Industry

Fish Farms: Besides the early quarry operation at the mouth of Indian Arm Inlet and the Wigwam Inn, there has been little or no industry in the inlet over the last fifty years. Attempts at fish farming are recorded here.

CHRONOLOGY—FISH FARMING

1985 Brothers Strato and Jim Malamas lease fish farm located at Orlomah Beach site from owner Tom Hopkins

1989 Silver Springs Aquaculture located south of Croker Island licensed for twelve pens

July 8 Five hundred chinook salmon smelts delivered to Pacific Aquaculture Ltd., the Malamas Corporation at Orlomah Beach

July Jim Malamas shot at with rifle by Klaus Krey while scuba diving at the Orlomah Beach fish farm site

August The DNV rescinds a former approval for Pacific Aquaculture to expand its facility from four to twenty fish pens

October Pacific Aquaculture moves its fish farm from Orlomah Beach site to 2 km (1.25 mi) North of Best Point to appease its complaining neighbours

November The DNV passes bylaw that fish farming is no longer an acceptable use inside parks, recreation and open-space zoned lands; this does not apply to pre-existing fish farms or government enhancement programs for wild fish stocks. There are no longer fish farms in Indian Arm

CHAPTER 3

Riverside East

Riverside East developed over a number of years as a single-family zoned neighbourhood accessed by Riverside Drive, a road built originally as a pipeline right-of-way to carry water from the upper Seymour River to Second Narrows and thence to the City of Vancouver. The neighbourhood extends north from Mount Seymour Parkway to the Seymour Canyon. Pedestrian access now extends into the Lower Seymour watershed as far as Twin Bridges and beyond. The Seymour Official Community Plan (OCP) of 1988 examined the possibility of extending development to the east up the slope as Riverside Terrace. However, later geotechnical studies favoured retaining the slopes for natural parkland.

Some of the original homes in the Seymour area are located in Riverside East. Early settlers found this idyllic spot and built log cabins by the riverside. The original rustic dwellings soon gave way to innovative, architecturally designed

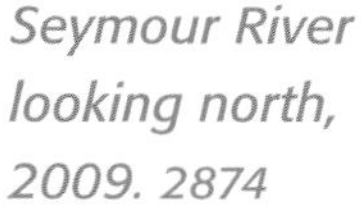

Seymour River looking north, 2009. 2874

Riverside neighbourhood, 1953. *Courtesy District of North Vancouver, 2790*

homes (necessitated by the terrain). Small developments appeared.

Residents shared a community spirit with their Maplewood neighbours. Local activities included horseback riding, parades and hiking the trails up to Pipeline Bridge. The children attended Maplewood Elementary School.

Former Riverside resident Eileen Curtis writes: "The Seymour River is a vivid entity, always within hearing especially at night. It is calm and cooling in summer with fishing, rafting, kayaking, paddling and swimming. In fall, winter and spring it roars, as rainfall fills the banks to near overflowing."

Riverside East is a piece of paradise tucked away in the tall trees, close to the rest of the North Shore and to the Ironworkers Memorial Second Narrows Crossing to Vancouver.

However, the steep hillside that defines the area has caused much grief over the years. Landslides have crashed down from the Blueridge neighbourhood perched above, eventually taking a life and the homes of many residents.

People

Terrance Darius "Doc" Hogan, 1902–82: The Hogan family was famous for its garden parties and garden tours. In the late 1940s, Doc Hogan developed a showpiece garden that he named Sharonvale. People would come from Vancouver to see this blissful place. He kept horses, ponies and exotic birds and a crocodile in one of the ponds got so big he had to give it to the Stanley Park Zoo. A resident anteater would run up and down the river.

Doc loved to go round the neighbourhood and give flowers from his garden

Above: Swans at Sharonvale gardens, 1951. Courtesy Sharon Hogan, 2851

Right: Riverside neighbourhood along Seymour River, 1992. Courtesy District of North Vancouver, 2773

Left: Doc Hogan in Sharonvale gardens, 1949. Courtesy Sharon Hogan, 2861

Middle: Doc Hogan talking to a crowd at the PNE grounds, ca. 1937. Courtesy Sharon Hogan, 2820

Bottom: Original tickets to the 505 Club, located at 505 Riverside Drive, 1940s. Courtesy Wendy Rasmussen, 1545

to everybody he met. A highly intelligent man with many interests, he was the original herbalist. He earned the nickname "The Medicine Man" because of his herbal remedies for all sorts of things. He also started a mail-order health food product company that he promoted at the Pacific National Exhibition for many years.

The Hogan family held fundraisers to help complete the building of the Seylynn Hall across the river from their place. The hall later became home to the Mount Seymour Lions Club and multiple other community groups.[28]

Arnold Rasmussen: Mr. Rasmussen purchased his house in 1948 from the people who owned the famous racehorse Sea Biscuit. It had been originally built as a summer guesthouse on the west side of the river. The Rasmussen family lived there until 1981 when the house was demolished to make way for the Mount Seymour Parkway extension over the Seymour River to the Upper Levels Highway.

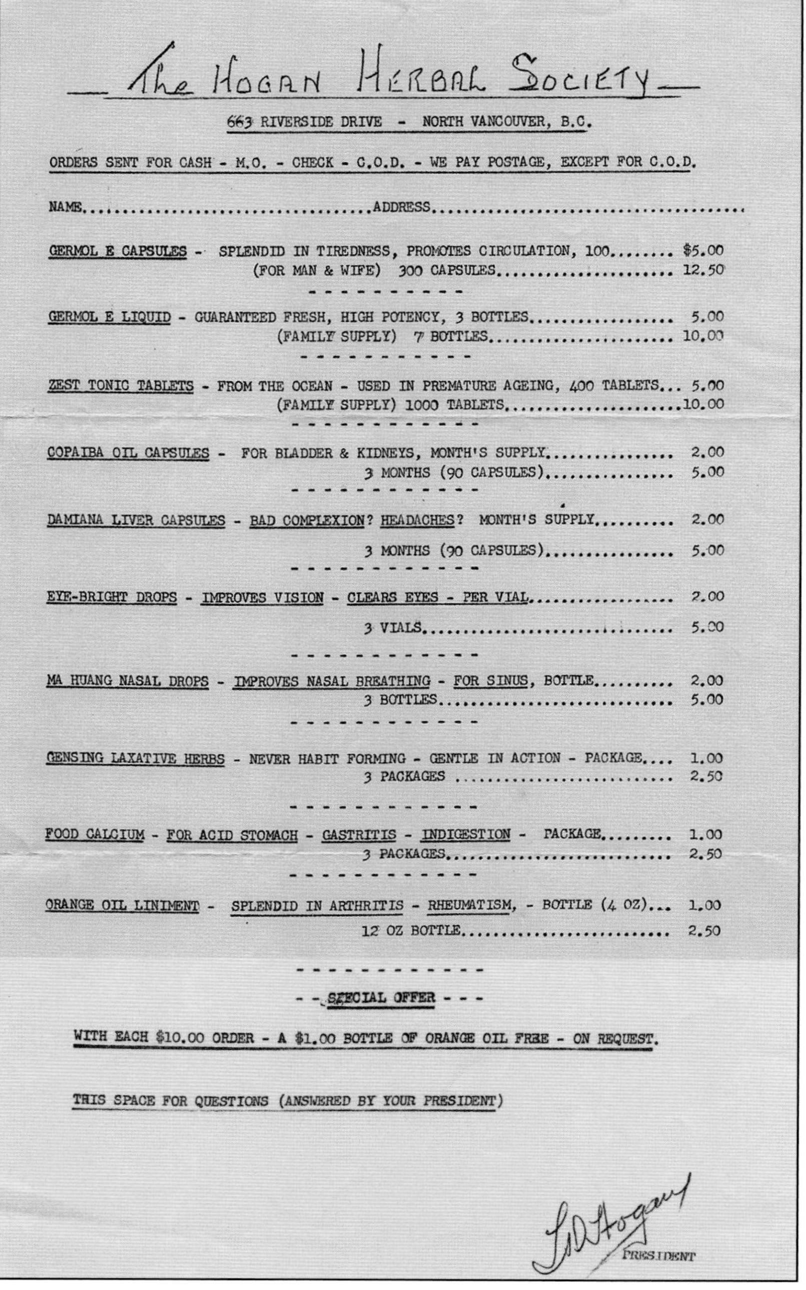

The Hogan Herbal Society

663 RIVERSIDE DRIVE - NORTH VANCOUVER, B.C.

ORDERS SENT FOR CASH - M.O. - CHECK - C.O.D. - WE PAY POSTAGE, EXCEPT FOR C.O.D.

NAME.................................ADDRESS.....................................

GERMOL E CAPSULES - SPLENDID IN TIREDNESS, PROMOTES CIRCULATION, 100........ $5.00
(FOR MAN & WIFE) 300 CAPSULES...................... 12.50

GERMOL E LIQUID - GUARANTEED FRESH, HIGH POTENCY, 3 BOTTLES.................. 5.00
(FAMILY SUPPLY) 7 BOTTLES........................ 10.00

ZEST TONIC TABLETS - FROM THE OCEAN - USED IN PREMATURE AGEING, 400 TABLETS... 5.00
(FAMILY SUPPLY) 1000 TABLETS......................10.00

COPAIBA OIL CAPSULES - FOR BLADDER & KIDNEYS, MONTH'S SUPPLY................ 2.00
3 MONTHS (90 CAPSULES)................ 5.00

DAMIANA LIVER CAPSULES - BAD COMPLEXION? HEADACHES? MONTH'S SUPPLY.......... 2.00
3 MONTHS (90 CAPSULES)................ 5.00

EYE-BRIGHT DROPS - IMPROVES VISION - CLEARS EYES - PER VIAL.................. 2.00
3 VIALS.............................. 5.00

MA HUANG NASAL DROPS - IMPROVES NASAL BREATHING - FOR SINUS, BOTTLE.......... 2.00
3 BOTTLES............................ 5.00

GENSING LAXATIVE HERBS - NEVER HABIT FORMING - GENTLE IN ACTION - PACKAGE.... 1.00
3 PACKAGES 2.50

FOOD CALCIUM - FOR ACID STOMACH - GASTRITIS - INDIGESTION - PACKAGE......... 1.00
3 PACKAGES........................... 2.50

ORANGE OIL LINIMENT - SPLENDID IN ARTHRITIS - RHEUMATISM, - BOTTLE (4 OZ)... 1.00
12 OZ BOTTLE......................... 2.50

- - SPECIAL OFFER - - -

WITH EACH $10.00 ORDER - A $1.00 BOTTLE OF ORANGE OIL FREE - ON REQUEST.

THIS SPACE FOR QUESTIONS (ANSWERED BY YOUR PRESIDENT)

L D Hogan
PRESIDENT

Above: The Hogan Herbal Society potions, 1950s. Courtesy Sharon Hogan, 2828

Top right: Sharon Hogan leads PNE Parade on horse. Courtesy Sharon Hogan, 2845

Mr. Rasmussen, who took pleasure in gambling during the late 1940s, owned the 505 Club, originally located in a barn on his property at 505 Riverside Drive, which is now 2104 Mount Seymour Parkway.

His daughter Wendy says: "It was funny—the address just kept changing." She remembers the family building a stage on top of a huge table, setting an old piano on top and putting on plays with her brother on the stage. Her mother later told her that the table was used for gambling.

Sharon Hogan: Sharon Porter, daughter of Doc Hogan, lives on the Seymour River in her father's original home. Riverside Drive was originally a gravel road called Pipeline and the Hogan's first address in 1941 was Pole 38 Pipeline Road. The large property stretched from the bottom of the old Snake Hill (now Windridge Drive) to Riverside Drive and included Hogan's Pools, which have now been taken over by the District of North Vancouver (DNV) as a protected area. At one time volunteers cleared some of the land for a children's baseball diamond.

It was an idyllic atmosphere to grow up in. There was skating on the Seymour River in the wintertime. A lot of snow fell in those days and Sharon and her brother each had a pony that they used to hook up to a sleigh. Horseback riding, hiking in the

Sharon Hogan being crowned Maplewood Queen. Left to right: Gail Milligan, Sandy Sutherland, Sharon Hogan, Donna Andrich and Wendy Wotten. Courtesy Sharon Hogan, 2842

woods and growing vegetables and fruit were the summer activities. As a young girl Sharon was crowned May Queen of Seylynn and participated in all the community parades. She eventually became an accomplished horsewoman and at the age of fourteen was chosen to lead the PNE parade, which she continued to do for the next twenty years.

Marilyn Baker, 1943–2006: In 1965 Dick and Marilyn Baker purchased .80 ha (2 acres) of land for $3,000 on Riverside and built their first home. It wasn't until 1979 that the road was paved.

Marilyn devoted most of her life to community service. She was instrumental in setting up Maplewood Daycare and Maplewood Childcare Centre. The school was housed in a log house purchased from Bill Van Lowan.

Mayor Marilyn Baker. Courtesy Dick Baker, 4725

Right: Michael Conway Baker. Courtesy Penny and Michael Conway Baker, 4490

Bottom: Christine Elsey. Courtesy Christine Elsey, 4532

She was also one of the founders of the Seymour Ratepayers Association, worked tirelessly on the Seymour Planning Association Committee and eventually, in 1982, became mayor of the DNV for an eight-year term. Even after retirement and a diagnosis of cancer, she was appointed to the Immigration and Refugee Board, the BC Ferry Board, the Law Enforcement Board and the Vancouver Port Authority.

Dick and Marilyn sailed the world in their yacht with their family on a year-and-a-half sabbatical, and eventually settled on Reid Island to enjoy a rustic lifestyle.

Marilyn was honoured many times over the years, including as the YWCA Woman of Distinction, vice-president of the Greater Vancouver Regional District, life member of the Union of BC Municipalities and Freeman of the District of North Vancouver in 2005. She was respected by all who knew her for her forthright and well-thought-out opinions, her honest approach and tireless dedication.

Michael Conway Baker: One of Canada's most successful composers, Michael Conway Baker is broad in his vision. From his Riverside Drive studio he has created more than 150 works for symphonies, concertos, film, television and both the National Ballet of Canada and the Royal Winnipeg Ballet. A member of the British Columbia Entertainment Hall of Fame, his awards include a Juno, a Gemini and three Genies, including one for his work on the film *The Grey Fox*, about BC railway bandit Bill Miner.

Themba Tana: Themba Tana, drum master and ethnomusicologist, was born in Cape Town, South Africa. He studied music at university there and in Zimbabwe before arriving in Canada in 1981. His presence immediately enlivened Vancouver's emerging world-beat scene, and through his wide travels he has become known as an educator in multicultural learning programs throughout Canada, the US and Japan.

"A Poetic Review of Seymour River Recollections"

—by Christine Elsey

The river is my blood, it is my arteries. It is the blood of my children and of my parents. For three generations we have lived on, and breathed the Seymour River.

The morning, hot steamy with a mild smell of salmon. A recollection from early childhood when the steelhead spawned so thick I could walk across on their backs. The occasional ponds of unscorched river—giving shining deathbeds to gasping fish.

And another season, then, at the canyon watching and weeping at the jumping humpbacks climbing the rapids to the spawning grounds above.

And then the river freezing over most years—as it never does now. The ice in those days went right across with just a black stream, of faster water, staying unfrozen. You could walk on that ice almost to the other bank. Almost to the woods to the place where the old black bear used to amble down for fish.

And some of my earliest recollections were of the hot rodders in the summer, careening up Riverside Drive to swim in the canyon pools—with their ducktail dos and brill cream waves—with their baffles pulled off and oh! What a sound! Jumped-up short beds, sometimes engines showing. Everyone with their chick, and they all went diving—big swan dives off the high cliffs, piercing deep into the frigid, green water.

And most of us kids would want to gawk. So our dads took us down to the cliffs in the boiling heat—to see them dive. A child under an armpit, picnic basket held tight, feet almost slipping on the steep, hot cliffs.

We all went to the canyon to get cool. River at my house dried to a trickle. Now all it was good for was for jumping rocks. Feet pure muscle—courage honed. Most big rocks were named but some of them weren't. Named rocks and jumping rocks, some hot, some shady—water skiers and minnows were fun to catch.

Every year the Seymour stayed the same in front of our house, small in summer, big in winter.

Every winter before the dam it raged and flooded homes. The dads went to sandbag one Christmas night. A house got carried down, by rapids, right to Maplewood—left high on the river's edge stuck up on a sandbank. It must have stayed there for a year.

A river is always stories and memories like the ghost town, above the canyon. A hermit, old Dinsdale, would lead us kids to see it.

Above twin bridges, it's still there, overgrown with salmonberries—right near "the elbow." There's a tunnel there too, a long one. That's up near the headwater.

At the front of our house, in the raging torrent, a neighbour girl fell in. Though only a girl, I dragged her back. Poor kid was too scared to cry.

Most years the river would stay the same—but one year there was a giant slide. The whole slope came down—slippery as jelly—with a noisy rumble it fell into the raging torrent just opposite our house.

Even the great snags came down snapping and crackling (the two great firs) that tangoed nightly with the little dipper—like silhouetted maidens on the top of the hill.

This is my river and a lot of other people's. It is our blood—their history—a continuity of perpetual stories—a flow of life whose flow is eternal.

Homes along the Seymour River, 1958. Courtesy Sharon Hogan, 2834

From his Riverside Drive home, Tana's percussive rhythms continue to communicate global harmony through his Drums for Compassion project work.

Environment

Riverside–Berkley Escarpment: Residents of the Seymour area are used to the rain—the DNV receives roughly 2,400 mm (95 in) annually. Nonetheless, the torrential downpour on the night of January 19, 2005, stands out in their minds.

Mount Seymour had seen over 200 mm (8 in) of rain the preceding week, with an additional 175 mm (7 in) that night. The groundwater levels in the Berkley–Riverside escarpment area finally reached breaking point at approximately 3:30 a.m. The fill-slope along the escarpment gave way to a landslide, and what followed was one of the largest recorded mass wastage events in Mount Seymour's history. Two homes were destroyed, causing one death and another critical injury.

Reaction to the slide was swift. The DNV firefighters, RCMP and North Shore Rescue were first on the scene, followed by Vancouver Urban Search and Rescue conducting its first-ever deployment.

Ultimately the debris was cleared, geotechnical engineers were hired by the DNV and high-risk levels were discovered in certain areas of the escarpment. The District implemented a buyout plan for the nine properties most severely affected by the landslide—properties that also carried potential risk in the case of future rainstorms. The bought-out houses were demolished and the area was developed into a green space.

Riverside mudslide, January 27, 1980. *Photo by Ian Smith,* North Shore News, *2653*

CHRONOLOGY—BERKLEY-RIVERSIDE ESCARPMENT

1940s Riverside East mainly a logging area

1950s Residential construction begins along the Berkley side of the Riverside escarpment

1960s Development of the Riverside area begins below the escarpment

1972–79 Five fill-slope failures are recorded including slide on December 21, 1979

1980s Storm sewer is finally constructed to divert runoff away from the slope. Still, many houses remained unconnected, allowing large amounts of water to course over the slope during times of high rainfall

2005 Fatal landslide occurs

Above: Berkley/ Riverside mudslide, 2005. Equipment and clean up at Berkley Avenue. *Courtesy North Shore Rescue, 2992*

Right: Mount Seymour and Seymour River. *Illustration by Adrian Germiquet, 1950, courtesy Wendy Rasmussen, 1549*

CHAPTER 4

Maplewood

Maplewood is the oldest neighbourhood in Seymour after the two First Nations' settlements: the Tsleil-Waututh on Thomas Creek and the Squamish on the west bank of Seymour Creek.

In 1865 Hugh Burr of New Westminster established the first farm in the area on 68 pre-empted hectares (169 acres) on the east bank of Seymour Creek. Burr sold the produce from his farm to other communities on Burrard Inlet and New

Maplewood area, 1953. Courtesy District of North Vancouver, 2778

Maplewood industrial area, 1971. Courtesy District of North Vancouver, 2750

Westminster. This land, together with later adjacent pre-emptions, became the heart of Maplewood.

The large District lots granted by the Crown to those pre-emptors who successfully met the requirements of the Land Act were, for the most part, subdivided into single-family residential lots early in the last century. In the 1930s these legal parcels of land were re-subdivided (and the roads renamed) to make way for the province to construct a new road, the Dollarton Highway, which was intended to open eastern Seymour for development.

The popular name of Maplewood was formally recognized when the Maplewood post office was established in the early 1940s.

Deeks Gravel Pit, 1950s (Note: building right of centre is the back of Accurate Iron Works, 2468 Dollarton Highway). Photo by Jack Cash, courtesy Joe Cubage, 2293

Industry

Deeks McBride Sand and Rock Company Limited: A trail leads toward Deeks Creek and Deeks Lake, both named after a rock and gravel company started by John F. Deeks in 1908 to service Vancouver construction. A small community of employees lived there and enjoyed good housing, a schoolhouse and tennis courts. The community was named Porteau (which roughly translated from the French means "water's gate").

A gravel airstrip, probably built during the Second World War, was used by private pilots until at least 1970, when the National Harbours Board had the rudimentary hangars demolished.

Allied Shipbuilders Ltd.: Founded in 1948 by T.A McLaren (1919–99), Allied Shipbuilders has built over 259 vessels during its nearly sixty years of continuous operation. Located at the mouth of the Seymour River in North Vancouver, the company provides shipbuilding, ship repair and engineering services to the commercial marine industry on the Pacific West Coast.

ERCO Worldwide: ERCO is one of the world's leading suppliers of sodium chlorate and bleaching technologies. Pulp mills use sodium chlorate to produce chlorine dioxide, which is used to bleach pulp for the manufacture of white paper products. ERCO operates six plants across Canada.

CHRONOLOGY—MAPLEWOOD

1860s First significant non-Native settlement

1800s to early 1900s Trees over 90 m (295 ft) in height and 11 m (36 ft) in circumference were logged; Windridge area extensively logged and several sawmills built along the waterfront

1865 Hugh Burr purchases first land east of Seymour River beginning first European settlement and logging industry

1930 Construction of the Dollarton Highway

1950s Port-oriented industry commences with first chemical plant

1960s Much vacant land plotted into large industrial parcels

1987 Ammonia runoff from duck pond results in high mortality of juvenile coho salmon

1990 First return of chum salmon following enhancement efforts[29]

2010 Industrial park is built to accommodate businesses and light industry

Construction of a sodium chlorate plant began in Maplewood in 1956. The plant was built on tidal flats and fill was brought in from Keith Road by truck and dredged fill was hydraulically pumped onto the flats from Burrard Inlet. The plant was expanded between 1965 and 1991 and with new technology the company positioned itself as a leading supplier. In 2007 ERCO Worldwide celebrated its fiftieth anniversary.

Hooker Chemicals: In the 1950s Canada's "Minister of Everything," C.D. Howe, invited the American firm Hooker Chemicals to build a chlorine manufacturing plant on Burrard Inlet to serve BC's growing paper industry. The Port of Vancouver would provide deep-sea access for ships bringing in bulk salt from Mexico; a new Walters substation would provide the vast amounts of electrical power needed in the chemical process; and the District of North Vancouver (DNV) together with the National Harbours Board would sell or lease Hooker Chemicals hundreds of

Allied Shipbuilders Ltd. at the mouth of the Seymour River. 2866

Above: Nova Lumber Mill in Maplewood before it burnt down. Photo by Desmond Smith, 1607

Left: View of industrial area from the Ironworkers Memorial Second Narrows Bridge, 2009. 2621

CHRONOLOGY—CHLORINE MANUFACTURING

1957 Hooker Chemicals plant starts up

1988 Becomes Canadian Oxy Chemicals

1995 Occidental Petroleum and Canadian Oxy Chemicals form a partnership and become known as CXY Chemicals

2000 CXY Chemicals changes its name to Nexen Chemicals

2005 Nexen Chemicals changes its name to Canexus Chemicals[30]

acres of intertidal lands that could be filled in to accommodate a new chemical plant, a railway yard and a sizeable security buffer zone. The project was an economic success for BC and the nation, but would prove to have long-term negative effects on the future development of Maplewood.

A group of concerned local residents formed the Chemical Hazards Alert Committee in the 1970s and met at the home of Arthur and Vivienne Coverdale.

ALS Laboratory Group: ALS has provided geochemical analysis in North Vancouver since 1967. ALS Group Mineral Division (formerly ALS Chemex) moved into its new, custom-built, geochemical analysis, assay and mineralogy laboratory in Maplewood in 2009, the largest and most advanced of its kind in the world.[31]

Rempel Brothers Concrete: In 1967 brothers Ewald, Ed and Clarence Rempel opened their first ready-mix concrete plant in Abbotsford. Their vision was to successfully meet the needs of the building community in their fast-growing town. They soon expanded to the North Shore and established a plant in Maplewood in the 1970s.[31]

Transfer Station and Recycling Drop-off Depot: The North Shore Transfer Station, 30 Riverside Drive, is operated by

The chlorine plant. (This company changed its name many times.) Courtesy Desmond Smith, 1603

North Van firm secures $30 million in submarine deals, 1987. "Christopher Metcalfe, general manager of Hyco Technologies Corp., displays scale model of the Aries transparent submersible soon to be manufactured on the North Shore. Two of the transparent submarines will be built for tourist use in Mexico." Photo by Neil Lucente, North Shore News, *3674*

Wastech Services Ltd. for residents, businesses and contractors to bring waste and yard trimmings. Items are screened for hazardous wastes and recyclable materials, loaded into large trucks and transferred to other facilities. The North Shore Recycling Drop-off Depot, 29 Riverside Drive, is a staffed, self-serve municipal recycling facility available to North Shore residents and small businesses for the drop off of larger volumes and sizes of materials.

Left: Rempel Brothers Concrete plant. 4521

Housing and Development

Mud Flats: In the 1970s a large hippie colony complete with very folksy dwellings thrived on the Maplewood mud flats. Unfortunately, it was a thorn in the side of the late mayor Ron Andrews and after several ignored demands to vacate the land, he ordered the District Fire Department to set the squatted houses ablaze.

Multi-use Town Centre: In the mid-1960s the National Harbours Board proposed construction of a major deep-sea terminal on the remaining intertidal lands. The proposed new terminal was to have the capacity to unload one hundred car-unit trains and store commodities such as coal, sulphur and potash prior to loading them onto ocean-going bulk carriers destined for the Asian market. Municipal manager Cyril Henderson travelled

Squatters' shacks in the Maplewood mud flats. Courtesy Janet Pavlik, 0857

to Ottawa and successfully opposed the project.

Council then commissioned the British firm of Grosvenor International to prepare a master plan for the development of "lands east of Lynn Creek," the name for the Seymour area at the time. Following the rejection of the 1970 Grosvenor Plan by citizens, staff and council, the District Planning Department was asked to prepare an Official Community Plan (OCP) for Seymour.

During preliminary public debate on redevelopment and transportation issues, agreement could not be reached between some residents of Seymour, Maplewood and Deep Cove. Council decided to proceed with separate OCPs for Maplewood and Deep Cove, prior to completing the Seymour OCP.

An earlier economic study had identified Maplewood as the preferred site for a town centre to serve all of Seymour. The Maplewood OCP adopted by council in mid-1983 included provisions for a multi-use town centre adjacent to and compatible with a protected conservation area.

Delays in the acquisition of a right-of-way across the Seymour Creek Reserve and in the construction of the Mount Seymour Parkway Bridge caused council to impose a moratorium on new development east of the Seymour River. The bridge was completed in 1984 and the Seymour OCP was finally adopted in November 1985.

Despite the interest expressed by three of Canada's largest commercial development companies, the proposed multi-use town centre project was put on hold until, through the efforts of Kevin Bell of the District of North Vancouver Parks Department, the District OCP of 1990 designated the multi-use centre's 25 ha (62 acres) of land and 22 ha (54 acres) of water to be part of an expanded Maplewood Conservation Area.

Schools

Maplewood Elementary School: The original Maplewood Elementary School opened in 1964. Florence Allardice recalls that it quickly became a magnet for families, who participated in anything they were asked to do. Florence introduced the Dewey decimal system into the library, along with a record and location of every book, a lengthy process. She remembers that the school concerts organized by the staff were always a joy.

Barbara Brown recalls that her mother borrowed equipment from the dairy farm across the street and taught the school children how to make butter.

When Maplewood was closed by the Board of Education in 2004 the building became home to Lions Gate Christian Academy, which operated a private school there until 2010.

The Kenneth Gordon Maplewood School, designed to help children with dyslexia and specific learning difficulties, presently operates from this location. The school accepts children between grades one and eight.

St. Simon's Church (Anglican Coalition in Canada) holds traditional and contemporary services and Sunday school in the

A sketch of Maplewood with Mount Seymour in the background, 1954. Location is NE corner of what is now Seymour River Place and Old Dollarton Road. Courtesy Wendy Rasmussen, 1547

Above: Maplewood Community School, Grade K Division 2, 1991-1992. Courtesy Asha Sehra, 3720

Right: Maplewood Elementary School staff, 1991–1992. Courtesy Asha Sehra, 3723

Left: Maplewood Preschool building. Courtesy Pat Morrice, 2134

school building under the direction of Reverend Ed Hird.

Canadian International College/Chung Dahm Immersion School: Built in 1988, Canadian International College was a joint venture of Nelson International School Inc. and Japanese business interests. The private school housed 1,200 Japanese students until 2004 when it was taken over by Chung Dahm International School, Vancouver. The school is a private boarding facility that offers English as a second language to Korean students in grades five to seven.

Merchants

The Maplewood area features over 300 small businesses. Some of the longest operating and most memorable were chosen to describe here.

Dial-A-Movie: In 1982 Celia and Raphael Buergler introduced video rentals to the Seymour area with a store on Mount Seymour Parkway. The couple opened three new stores between 1984 and 1993 at Maplewood, Dollarton and Parkgate, adding TV sales and service to the business.

With the demise of video and DVD rentals in the 2000s they had closed all locations by 2010.

The Crab Shop: The Crab Shop's humble beginnings lie with Fred Landry, a Nova Scotian who began crab fishing Coal Harbour in 1931 and founded the Crab Shack in 1951. For the Landrys crabbing was a family affair. His stepsons Sonny, Bill and Ed Dobay boiled and shucked crabs over driftwood fires on

Bottom: Dollarton Crab Shack before demolition, near the mudflats, ca. 1970s. DHCS, 0494

CHRONOLOGY—CRAB SHOP

1951 Crab Shack founded by Fred Landry

1984 September 30 Crab Shack at 2817 Dollarton Highway closes indefinitely

December 18 Grand reopening of the Dollarton Crab Shop at its new 2464 Dollarton Highway location

1986 December 26 Crab Shop owner Sonny Dobay's boat, *Barkley Surge*, is vandalized, released from its moorings in Deep Cove and submerged

1988 Vandals use eleven pounds of dynamite to cause explosion at the Crab Shop

1993 Crab Shop ownership taken over by Marcel Gregori

2004 Fire ravages the Crab Shop and almost demolishes the building

2007 Crab Shop relocated the third time, to the Kingswood Landing Development, 121–2455 Dollarton Highway

2009 Crab Shop attracts hordes of visitors for its famous fish and chips. The likes of Cindy Crawford, Arnold Schwarzenegger and Michael Bublé have dined here

the Maplewood mud flats. They opened a little shack that rested on floats at the end of a plank walkway, stilted across the flats. The operation was then taken over by Shirley and Sonny Dobay, who moved the shop to higher ground at its 2817 Dollarton Highway location. It operated there successfully until the property owners went bankrupt, and a housing developer bought the land.

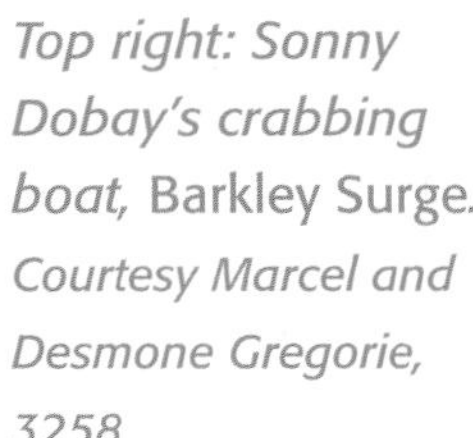

Top right: Sonny Dobay's crabbing boat, Barkley Surge. *Courtesy Marcel and Desmone Gregorie, 3258*

Right: Sonny Dobay surveys the damage done to the Crab Shop after vandals set off dynamite, destroying $50,000 worth of seafood processing equipment. Photo by Neil Lucente, North Shore News, *2993*

Amadeus Family Hair Salon: In 2008 owner–operators George and Dennise Semora celebrated twenty years in their Maplewood location—quite a record, as so many businesses in the area did not survive. When asked the significance of the name Amadeus, George answered with a story from his boyhood town of Brno, Czechoslovakia. In the library where he would study, he noticed a plaque claiming that Wolfgang Amadeus Mozart had composed several symphonies in that very place. When he started his business in Maplewood he thought what a nice reminder of Europe it would be to name his salon Amadeus.

Blueridge–Cove Animal Hospital: Dr. Moe Milstein, BSc, DVM, DipMed, has been with the Blueridge–Cove Animal Hospital since 1979, during which time he spent fifteen years as the official vet for the Vancouver Police Dog Squad.

Jolly Meats: Marion Segner opened this popular European meat and delicatessen store in the 1960s. Known as a traditional butcher shop, it also has a good selection of Scandinavian deli and groceries. Eric Esmann has been working at Jolly Meats since the beginning. The present owner is Lugie de Mutiis.

Above: Blueridge-Cove Animal Hospital. 2628

Arts and Culture

Artie George and Richard de la Mare: On March 11, 1970, Richard and his wife rented the house on Dollarton Highway that many years later was to become Coast

Botttom: Maplewood Plaza merchants, 2009. 3678

Raven Design Studio. For forty years Richard has worked as a visual artist in various mediums, but his particular interest is jewellery.

When Richard's great-aunt bequeathed her bead collection to him, he was determined to make good use of the antique beads. Richard became known as the Bead Man in Vancouver.

"I made them for belly dancers, I made them for powwow dancers and I made them for singers," he said.

Richard grew up and spent a lot of time with the Artie George family on the nearby Indian reservation. A lifelong association in art developed between the men. Artie George has gone on to become a renowned Native artist. He graduated from Seycove Secondary School, where he attended Native art classes. His love of carving is reflected in the small, one-of-a-kind pieces that are featured in art shops throughout the Lower Mainland.

Above: Artie George and Richard de la Mare outside their former studio, 2008. 1071

Right: Silverwork by Richard de la Mare. 3683

Below: Frog carved by Artie George. 2909

Recreation

Maplewood Farm: Officially opened to the public in 1975 and now home to over 200 domestic animals and birds, Maplewood Farm strives to provide a unique

Above: Maplewood Farm, 2009. 2648-07

experience, incorporating enjoyment, education and a recollection of the rural heritage of this pastoral five-acre setting.

CHRONOLOGY—MAPLEWOOD FARM

1900s Mr. Akiyo Kogo discovers this idyllic little spot

1924–44 Mr. Joseph Ellis starts a dairy business

1944 John and Helen Smyth buy the dairy farm. A portion of the property fronting on Seymour Boulevard was later sold to Betty and Don Brown

1946 John Smyth starts a dog training and boarding business

1964 Robert and Rita McClung operate a dog boarding/training facility

1970 The farmland comes under the protection of the District of North Vancouver Parks department

Left: Katie Boughen feeding goats at Maplewood Farm, 2009. 2648-38

North Shore Riding Stables, 1971–80: North Shore Riding Stables was a hive of activity in Maplewood. Operators John and Florence Lattin held riding lessons, barn dances and gymkhanas. They put on benefit performances in aid of crippled children (now Lions Society for Children with Disabilities) and did rehab with children with disabilities by teaching them to ride horses. Chief Dan George of the Tsleil-Waututh was featured in a movie filmed on the property.

Florence Allardice recalls: "One little boy who came to the riding stables couldn't walk. He had a body brace, braces on his shoulders and both legs. We

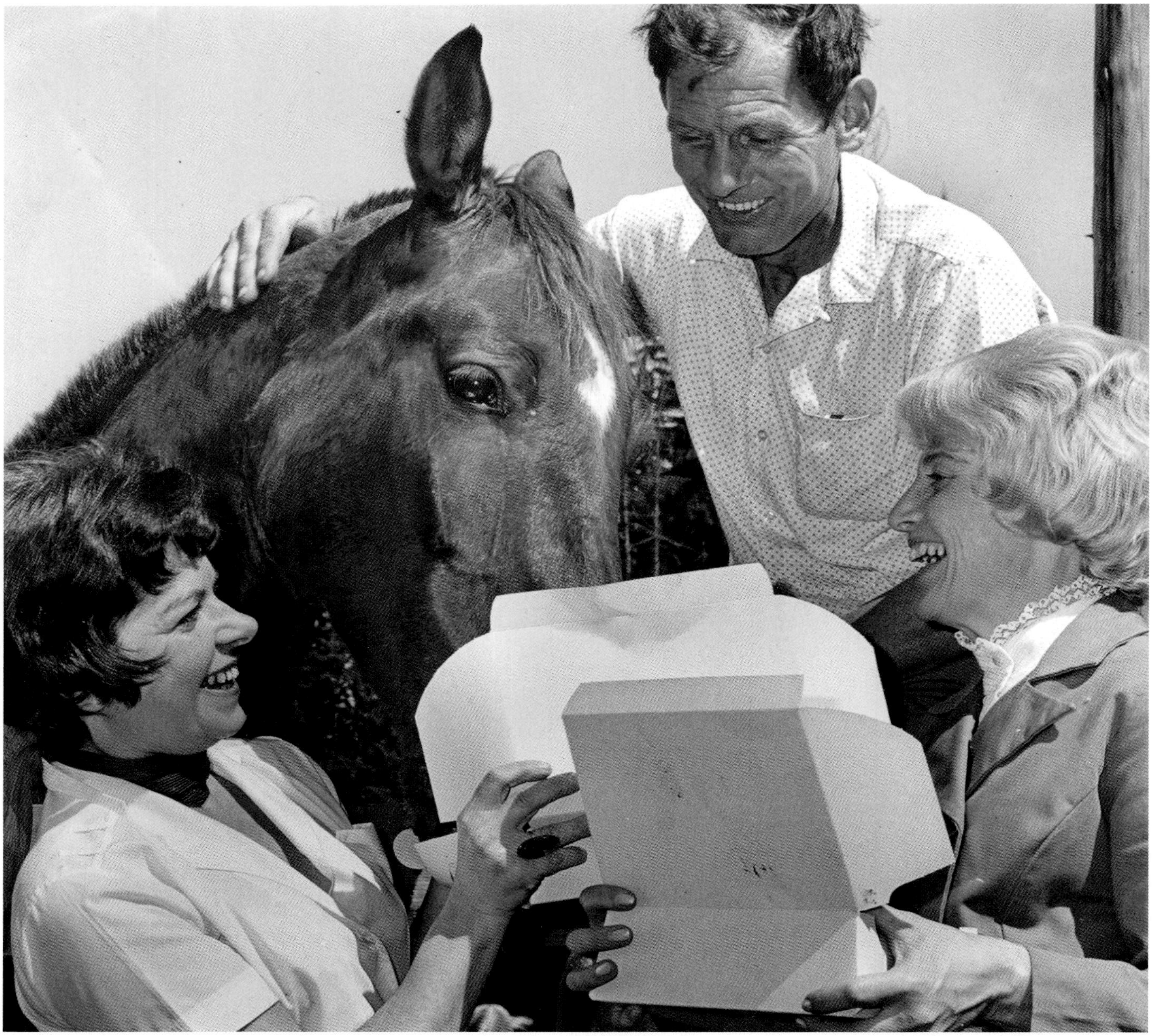

Florence and John Lattin, and Mrs. Blackhall, ca. 1975. *Courtesy Florence Lattin-Allardice, 1282*

removed his braces and helped him into a harness on the horse. He was so happy and excited to be up there riding. Two school kids helped keep him from falling by leading the horse.

"It was a hot sunny day and the little boy was on the large, gentle plough horse called Ed. Well, Ed decided to go for a swim. Into the water he went; there was the little boy floating up from Ed's body. The girls on both sides dove in and swam beside him. They reined in the horse and rescued the little boy who was yelling, 'Momma, look at me!' with the biggest grin on his face."

Environment

Maplewood Creek Watershed: The Maplewood Creek part of the Seymour River system originates above Mount Seymour Parkway. Groundwater from upslope terraces discharges through several springs and seepages and supports a network of wetlands that form the headwaters. The water quality has degraded due to riparian removal, urbanization and culvert building.[32] The residents of Maplewood worked with the District staff to create a Maplewood Local Plan that incorporated the environmental, social and economic values of the District OCP while still addressing the expressed needs of the Maplewood community.

Having completed their local plan in 2002, the residents carried on to explore the concept of community sustainability in a green project aimed at solving many of the environmental problems generated by earlier industrial development. The results of the study were published as *The Maplewood Project* in 2004.

Environment Canada: The first municipal planner for the DNV, Martin Chesworth, asked the federal government to do a detailed environmental study of their intertidal lands. These Crown lands were not under the control of the municipality. The study findings became a turning point in the future planning for the waterfront lands. The intertidal lands and foreshore were judged to be vital wild bird habitat on the North American Pacific Flyway and also a very important rearing area for

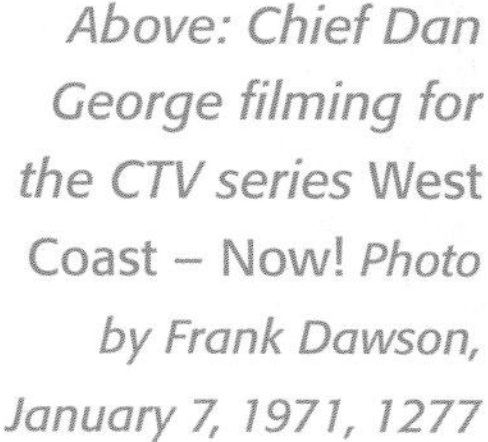

Above: Chief Dan George filming for the CTV series West Coast – Now! *Photo by Frank Dawson, January 7, 1971, 1277*

Left: A bear cub scampers after his mother across the busy Dollarton Highway, 1981. Photo Ian Smith, North Shore News, *3036*

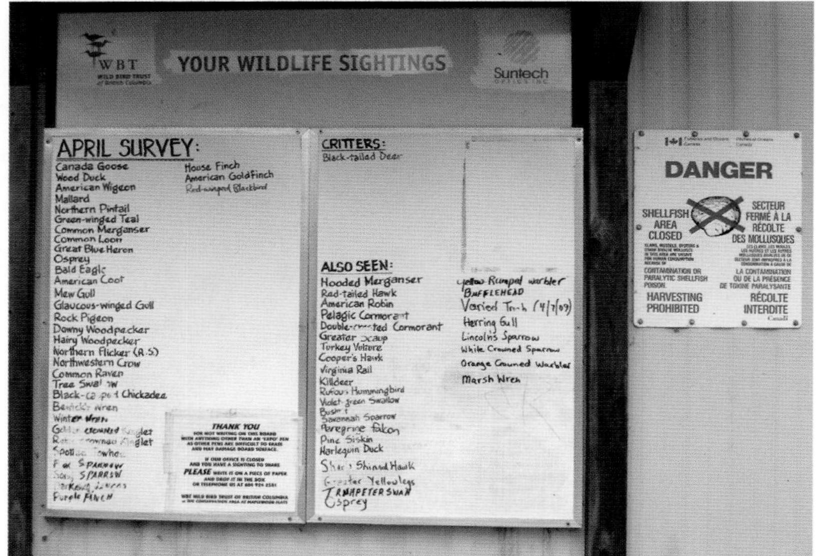

Top: American Goldfinch. Photo by Damon Calderwood, 2935

Above: Wild bird sightings board in the Maplewood Conservation Area. 2582

young Pacific salmon. The study done by Environment Canada and the Fisheries and Marine Service complemented the background research being done by District staff in the preparation of the Seymour OCP.

Environment Canada located its new regional laboratory on the site. A wild bird trust was created to take over management of the conservation areas, and it was open to public viewing under supervision.

Wild Bird Trust

The Maplewood Conservation Area in North Vancouver is the last undeveloped waterfront wetland on the north shore of Burrard Inlet. For over twenty years public interest groups lobbied to preserve this prime site as a wildlife sanctuary. In 1992 the owners of the majority of the area (the federal government's Vancouver Port Authority, or VPA) reached an agreement to lease the VPA area for forty-nine years to Environment Canada to be managed as a wildlife conservation area. The VPA, the DNV and Environment Canada chose Wild Bird Trust (WBT) of British Columbia as the operators of the conservation area. The WBT is a non-profit, membership-based provincial organization founded in 1993 by Dr. Richard C. Beard and Patricia M. Banning-Lover.

Dedicated to the protection of birds and their habitats, the WBT turned a former degraded industrial site into a haven for wildlife—a "living classroom" for all to enjoy.[33]

CHAPTER 5

Windridge

Windridge was originally known as Snake Hill, where Keith Road snaked its way up from the floodplain of Seymour Creek to the Seymour Heights plateau. With the construction of the new Mount Seymour Parkway by the province along a more direct route, the old Keith Road route was renamed Windridge Drive at the suggestion of Ruth Mitchell, a local resident. An earlier economic study had recommended that if a full town centre was not to be built in Maplewood then

Windridge and Maplewood areas, 1971. Courtesy District of North Vancouver, 2751

Windridge, old Deeks Quarry and Windsor Park areas, 1992. Courtesy District of North Vancouver, 2766

two community level shopping centres should be built, one in the east (Parkgate) and one in the west (Windridge).

After council decided not to build a town centre in lower Maplewood, area proposals were made to develop a Windridge centre in a village style, with small shops and a variety of low-, medium- and high-density housing, a new park, medical services and recreation facilities. Berkley Avenue was to be extended downhill to intersect with a realigned Dollarton Highway. In a series of separate decisions, much of the available land in Windridge was used up by the expansion of the recreation centre parking, a youth centre and a major ice arena with extensive parking. With the opening of a Superstore on the Seymour Creek Reserve to the west, the future of Windridge will probably be limited to residential and park development.

Housing and Development

The Dalton Home: The Dalton family purchased their home at 2353 Windridge Drive in 1967. According to Lynda Dalton,

Left: Browning Place, 2009. 2884

Bottom left: The Dalton family home at 2353 Windridge Drive. 2880

Bottom right: Swimming pool and apartments at Seymour Estates, 2009. 3024

it was originally built in the mid-1950s by Emma Cameron and her husband and was one of the first Pan-Abode homes in North Vancouver. When it was built the home was located along the original Snake Hill, which later became Windridge Drive. It sits atop the Windridge escarpment and afforded the Daltons a view of Burrard Inlet and Capital Hill as well as Grouse Mountain to the northwest.

In 1974 the Daltons completed a two-bedroom addition and relocated the original Pan-Abode garage to the backyard. The garage came to be known as "The Shack at the Back." It served as both a workshop and a gathering spot for the neighbourhood's youth. Several other alterations to the home including a solarium and deck were made before the Daltons sold the property in 2004.

Seymour Estates: Seymour Estates at 904, 916 and 940 Lytton Street comprises three strata managed buildings. The 940 and 916 buildings were built in 1969 and both contain 116 units. The 904 building was built as a 115-unit addition the following year.

Kiwanis Care Centre: The Kiwanis Club of North Vancouver received its founding charter in 1921 and in 1951 their housing branch, Kiwanis Senior Citizens Homes Limited, was founded. In 1992 the BC Ministry of Health allotted funds to build a new multi-level care facility and a site at 2444 Burr Place in Windridge was chosen. A lease with the District of North Vancouver (DNV) was signed in 1993 and design work began. The 192-bed Kiwanis Care Centre residential facility was officially opened by Minister of Health Penny Priddy on March 28, 1998. The centre is currently operated by Vancouver Coastal Health and North Shore/Coast Garibaldi Health Services under the mandate of providing a holistic and individualized approach to resident care.

Schools

Windridge Park Preschool:

Owner–operator Jan Argent recalls:

> The year was 1985, and my friend and Early Childhood Education colleague, Diane Prescott, and I were envisioning operating our own play-based preschool in the East Seymour Area of North Vancouver. This was the same year that the North Vancouver Recreation Commission was planning new facilities at the Ron Andrews Recreation Centre and in September of 1986 Windridge Park Preschool opened its doors in the brand new facilities at Ron Andrews.

Left: Kiwanis Care residents and care workers. Courtesy Janet Pavlik, 1519

Opposite top left: Kiwanis Care Centre, 2009. 2888

Opposite top right: Centre under construction. Courtesy Janet Pavlik, 1526

Opposite bottom: Evergreen Kiwanis Club members. Courtesy Janet Pavlik, 1527

Seymour Youth Centre: In 1990 a group of parents concerned about rising teen violence and drug abuse levels in the Seymour area came together to form the Seymour Area Youth Services Society (SAYSS). Subsequently the Mount Seymour Lions Club decided to partner with SAYSS in lobbying for a new youth centre in the Seymour area. In 1991 the DNV passed a rezoning bylaw allowing the centre to be built on undeveloped lands west of Ron Andrews Recreation Centre.[34] The two-storey, 250-sq-m (2,700-sq-ft) building was eventually built on its current site at 949 Lytton Street, and was opened in 1991.

Graffiti mural, spelling "knowledge," inside the Seymour Youth Centre, 2009. 3003

Recreation

Ron Andrews Recreation Centre: During the 1970s local citizens began lobbying for more recreation facilities east of Lynn Creek. On December 12, 1972, the taxpayers approved a Parks and Recreation bylaw, which allowed for the construction of an indoor swimming pool in the Seymour area.

Initially it was proposed that the new pool be constructed in conjunction with a new physical education complex, as an addition to Windsor Secondary School. Land adjacent to the school was pegged as the potential site for the proposed educational-recreational facility. However, this proposal did not go forward and the pool was subsequently built on its current site at 913 Lytton Street.

The official opening of Ron Andrews Pool as the first major public recreation facility built in the Seymour area took place on July 9, 1975. The new swimming pool provided much-needed swim classes to an area that abounds in local beaches. Prior to Ron Andrews Pool, residents had to travel to the North Vancouver Recreation Centre.

In the 1980s Ron Andrews Pool closed for renovations and expansion. The grand re-opening of Ron Andrews Recreation Centre on July 6, 1987, showcased the new 743-sq-m (8,000-sq-ft) addition, which

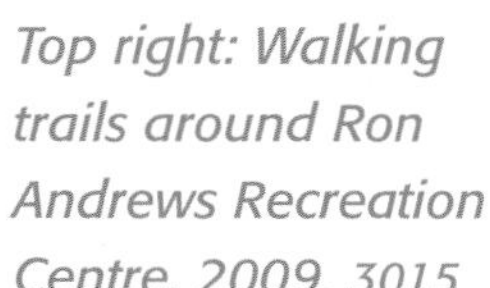

Top right: Walking trails around Ron Andrews Recreation Centre, 2009. 3015

Below: Ron Andrews Pool with mural of the Seymour area by Cristina Peori. Courtesy Cristina Peori, 4449–192

included an activities room, plus racquetball and squash courts. A preschool room, indoor playground, youth lounge and extra parking were also constructed at this time.

Since its opening, the rec centre has fostered many arts, culture and fitness programs. A mural of the entire Seymour area was painted on the walls of the pool area by artist Cristina Peori. The mural offers swimmers a graphic reminder of the Seymour area's natural beauty.

North Shore CHENA Team: The Mount Seymour Swim Team was formed in 1976 and merged with Lions Gate Swim Team on March 26, 1979.[35] In 1980 the name was changed to CHENA Swim Club "in order to better reflect the heritage of our region." One member recalls an early meeting of the amalgamated clubs: "A high-profile member of our First Nations was on the executive and he suggested 'Chena,' a Coast Salish word for salmon. Hence the First Nations motif of a salmon as the club symbol. Later we were told there is no such word in Coast Salish, though there is a Chena River in Alaska." CHENA is a member of Swim BC and Swimming Canada, the provincial and national governing bodies. Some of the CHENA swimmers who have met with success at senior national, collegiate or international levels over the years include:

Kathleen Stoody: Undefeated in the National Association of Intercollegiate Athletics (NAIA) competitions for Simon Fraser University, Kathleen went on to compete as a member of the Canadian national team, winning silver and bronze medals at the 2003 Pan Am Games and taking NAIA Swimmer of the Year honours in 2004.

Playground outside Ron Andrews Recreation Centre, 2009. 2897

Michelle Landry: Michelle was a member of Canada's national swim team from 2002–08. She was a finalist in the International University Sports Federation's World University Games in 2003, 2005 and 2007; a multiple medallist at various national championships; is a multiple provincial and national record holder; and was named 2007 North Shore Female Athlete of the Year.

Laura Jensen: Laura competed for Canada at the Beijing Paralympic Games in 2008, where she was a finalist in four events, finishing sixth in both the 50-metre and 100-metre freestyle in her category. She is the Canadian record holder in her category in the 100-metre and 200-metre backstroke.

Canlan Ice Sports: In 1992 the DNV formed a Seymour Facility and Services Review Committee that introduced a survey of the recreational needs of the Seymour area. The number one request by Seymour residents was an ice rink. The DNV initially ignored the request, even

Right: Interior of the Canlan Ice Sports building. Photo by Whitney Spearing, 4380

Bottom: Seymour Dance performers. Courtesy Sonia Ellis, 4774

though parents were literally camping out overnight at the Lonsdale Recreation Centre in order to enrol their children in youth hockey programs. The North Vancouver Minor Hockey Association and Seymour area residents began to lobby and petition for the DNV to address the need for an ice rink in Seymour.[36]

Ultimately the ice rink proposal was acted upon and a deal struck with Canlan Ice Sports, a large private sector operator of sixty-two recreational ice facilities across North America. The site at 2411 Mount Seymour Parkway was chosen for the facility due to its ease of access, level grade and close proximity to other recreational facilities. The four-rink facility was completed in 1998 and contains three NHL-sized ice surfaces and an additional smaller practice surface. Canlan Ice Sports facility plays host to several large-scale hockey events and tournaments. The building also houses the Thirsty Penguin Grillhouse restaurant, Ultimate Sports Store, the Hockey Performance Centre and Little Orchard Daycare.[37]

Seymour Dance Studio: Seymour Dance has operated in the Seymour area for over forty years. The school's original facility was in the Seymour Heights Community Hall and is now located at 808 Lytton Street. The school has turned out world-renowned dancers and teachers such as Teya Wilde (former student and teacher at Seymour Dance). Wilde was a top-twenty-two contender on the televised dance competition, *So You Think You Can Dance Canada*. The studio continues its long-standing Christmas season tradition of performing *The Nutcracker* at Centennial Theatre on Lonsdale. Seymour Dance is currently owned by Sonia Ellis of the Royal Academy of Dance. Her business was voted the number-one North Vancouver dance school for 2010 by the *North Shore Outlook*.[38]

Above: Darren Perkins sculpting "Gentlefolk" mugs, ca. 1978. Courtesy Darren Perkins, 2913

People

Darren Perkins: Darren and Susan Perkins started Windridge House Pottery in September 1977, after moving to Windridge Drive. Their handcrafted, bearded and mustached face mugs were sold through the Hudson's Bay Company Canadiana gift shop. Their next creation, Gentlefolk, was stoneware character figures that became very popular and were sold all over BC and eventually in stores across Canada.[39]

Left: "Gentlefolk" figurines by Windridge House Pottery. Courtesy Darren Perkins, 2914

CHAPTER 6

Seymour Heights

Where does Seymour Heights end and Blueridge begin? Seymour Heights is by far the older neighbourhood of the two, with some of its southerly development being traced back to the early days of the District of North Vancouver (DNV) in 1912. Blueridge was developed much later. Both neighbourhoods experienced considerable growth in the 1960s. The northern extension of

Seymour Heights and Riverside/ Blueridge. Courtesy District of North Vancouver, 2772

Seymour Heights. *Courtesy District of North Vancouver, 2746*

Seymour Heights was built by the District only after draining a large swamp that had deterred further development over the years. When the first construction equipment entered the area from Emerson Way, it uncovered a late-model Buick automobile that had sunk completely into the Seymour Heights swamp.

The newly serviced lots in Seymour Heights were offered to the public on an individual sealed bid basis. Spurred on by the District's radio advertising, the sale of the new lots was soon bringing in bids as high as those received on similar lots in the western District. The fact the new lots in Seymour Heights were only twenty minutes from downtown Vancouver over the new Second Narrows Bridge had a very positive influence on their market value.

Housing and Development

Seymour Heights has a superior suburban atmosphere which was created in the beginning and has been maintained. The Blueridge Garden Apartments located at 900–912 Berkley Road and 989 Lytton Street were built in 1968. The Berkley Terraces apartment complex (31 units) was built in 1989 and is located at 999 Berkley Road.

Right: Seymour Heights. *Courtesy District of North Vancouver GIS Department, 3308*

Below: Berkley Terraces condominium complex, ca. 2011. *Photo by Whitney Spearing, 4377*

Schools

Seymour Heights Elementary School: Seymour Heights Elementary School (2640 Carnation Street) was built in 1958. The 2010–11 school year statistics showed 199 students enrolled under principal Doug Beveridge.[40] The Seymour Heights Parent Advisory Council (PAC) is heavily involved with the running of the school and provides funds for all classroom supplies including paper, books and art materials. The PAC also hosts events, sports and cultural programs and recently funded two new school playgrounds.[41]

Over the years the gym at Seymour Heights Elementary has been used for a variety of community purposes, including exercise classes. Participants recall the aerobics instructor, Gail Honey, wife of Rick Honey, a long-time host of a daily radio show on CKNW. Gail's class often included well-known personalities such as CBC's Vicki Gabereau.

Seymour Heights Elementary School class photo, grade 5, division 5, ca. 1967. Courtesy Margaret Roberge, 4012

Seymour Heights Elementary School class photo, grade 1, division 9, 1962–63, teacher Sylvia Ziola. Courtesy Michael Thorpe, 4524

Seymour Heights Community Hall: Few people in the Seymour/Blueridge area today remember the community hall located half a block west of Emerson on Mount Seymour Parkway. Made entirely of wood, high-ceilinged, almost chapel-like, it stood and served the community in the 1970s and 1980s as a preschool and dance studio.

In less sophisticated times the playground at the back of the hall consisted of log structures, pulleys, sand, a tree fort and a natural environment for exploration, experimentation and curiosity. Maintenance both inside and out was taken care of by the parents. The rustic playground would no doubt be considered unsafe by today's standards but it served the preschool children and their families well.

In 1989 the building itself was condemned and vacated by its tenants. Today houses sit on the land where the community hall once stood. Jane Allen says, "As I walk past, my wish is that in our crowded world, there will always be spaces in our community where families can work and play and support each other in order to better manage the task of educating and guiding their children through their formative years."

Jane Allen at Seymour Heights Community Hall with advertising for Seymour Heights Parent Participation Preschool. Courtesy Jane Allen, 1941

Merchants

Chevron: The Chevron station that currently stands at 2620 Mount Seymour Parkway at the corner of Lytton Street is not the original building that housed the gas station. In 1967 Standard Oil of BC and contractor Wescan Ltd. began building the original Chevron station. In 1994 the building was demolished to make way for a new structure, which had its peak and clock feature over the front door added in 1999. In 2000 a business licence was issued to the Town Pantry at the Chevron.

Seymour Heights Store: The residents of Seymour Heights share fond memories of the small corner store at the corner of Emerson Way and Mount Seymour Parkway. Windsor Secondary students used to linger there on the way home from school to buy five-cent candies, smoke cigarettes and play popular arcade games. But then the store was boarded up, to the dismay of the owner Carmelita Chan, who says the business had been in her family for three generations. In 2011 the store is still boarded up, but the parking lot has become home to a seasonal fresh berry stand in the summer months.

People

Kerry Baxter: Kerry Baxter recalls coming to Seymour Heights as a small boy in 1948 from the United Kingdom. At the time the area was very rural and full of small chicken farms. His father, Hedley Scott Baxter, had married a war bride, Ethel, in 1942, and had gone to work at the Deeks gravel pit. Kerry's mother was quite dismayed upon arriving in Seymour to find herself in a two-room, 37-sq-m (400-sq-ft) ski shack with an outhouse and chicken coop.

Having no running water and heating water on the stove to fill a large portable tin tub made life all the more rustic and difficult. Kerry remembers Saturday night as family bath night. He was the last in the tub so he got to "pee" in the water that was later chucked out.

Kerry also tells of Greer's Store, which later became the community hall, home to badminton games, Christmas pageants and ballet classes.

The Thorpe Family: In September 1961, Michael Thorpe placed a bid on a house and lot located at the northeastern corner of Berkley Road and Belloc Street. The house and four surrounding properties were owned at the time by a Mrs. Bidwell. Michael Thorpe succeeded in purchasing the lot for $2,900. He recalls that when the family first moved in there was a turkey farm and sheds located just down from his property on the opposite side of Berkley Road.

Above: Herbert George of the Burrard Reservation clearing the Thorpe family property at Belloc Street with his two horses, Blackie and Whitey, 1962. Photo by Sedawie, Vancouver Sun, *4416*

Left: Thorpe family in front of their home, ca. 1963. Courtesy Michael Thorpe, 4415

CHAPTER 7

Blueridge

Early development in Blueridge had been done by a private developer. Later, waist-deep water and mud did not deter the District construction surveyors, and soon, extensions of both Berkley and Hyannis had been paved and underground wiring installed, followed by the development of adjacent local roads connecting the two neighbourhoods.

A private developer (reportedly from Hayseed, Texas) had built the early southern and eastern parts of Blueridge. His

Blueridge, 1953. Courtesy District of North Vancouver, 2792

Blueridge, 1971. Courtesy District of North Vancouver, 2756

private ownership of the Blueridge water supply was contested and had to be resolved by a very rare use of District powers of expropriation before the new northern and western expansion of Blueridge could be serviced by the municipality. The new residents of western Blueridge (living in their modern homes, close to Canada's third-largest city) have on nights of a full moon, experienced the mournful calls of wild coyotes gathered across the river on the Inter River Plateau beneath the great white cross of the cemetery as it was bathed in the moon's eerie blue glow. This is a truly unique Blueridge experience and is well in keeping with the spirit of the District planning goal: "Harmony with Nature."

Schools

Blueridge Elementary School: Blueridge Elementary is located at 2650 Bronte Drive, and was built in 1968 with an open-area concept. Many areas of the building had been divided into separate classrooms, but a semi-open area remains. In 2009 a total of 312 students enrolled at Blueridge, which offered a vibrant music program from kindergarten to grade seven, including choir and band. Students also enjoyed a wide variety of extracurricular athletic opportunities sponsored and coached by staff members and parents.[42]

Staff and students worked in partnership with the parent community through the Blueridge Parent Advisory Council (BPAC), which provided funds to support peer counselors, grade six first aid training and student recognition programs. Traditional events hosted by BPAC and the school included the Welcome Back Barbeque, Newcomer's Tea, Family Bingo Night and Fun Day.[43] BPAC also provided generous financial support for key school initiatives and made sizable investments into school playground equipment. In 2011 the North Vancouver School Board closed the school due to decreased elementary school enrollment in the area.

Community and Events

Blueridge Community Association: The Blueridge Community Association (BCA) was founded in October 1992 by members Bob Donoghue, Ernie Schmidt, Alex Volpatti, Randy Crighton, Jim Arthurs, Stephen Parker and Dave Hewitt. Eric Andersen, current chair of the BCA, explains that the group initially came together over concerns regarding a proposed Hyannis Connector road that would link to Lynn Valley, adding more traffic and bringing more development through the untouched forest west of Blueridge. They took their concerns to the District

Blueridge Elementary School, 2008. Ryan Crocker Photography, 2611–05

of North Vancouver council and the connector was never built. In 1995 their attention was turned to the proposed development project in both Cove and Mountain forests.

The BCA holds regular meetings open to all residents of Blueridge. Its mandate is to enhance livability for the residents of the area. BCA's regular activities include co-hosting all-candidates' meetings prior to every municipal, provincial and federal election, and publishing a couple of newsletters per year for residents. It also organizes the hugely popular annual Blueridge Good Neighbour Day, which started in 1998 and continues on today.[44] The event is held at Blueridge Elementary School and is supported by student and parent volunteers and community members.

Blueridge Community Association logo. 3297

Good Neighbour Day has had a different theme every year, such as Superheroes and Olympic Spirit. Over the years the day has included the Blueridge parade, dunk-tanks, pony rides, panning for gold and other community-oriented events.

Blueridge Elementary School class photo, grade 7, division 1, 1996–97. Courtesy Whitney Spearing, 3959

Right: Wet sponge toss at Blueridge Elementary School, 2008.

Below: RCMP members with Olympic mascot Quatchi, 2009.

Photos by Michelle McKnight, courtesy Blueridge Community Association, 4420, 4421

People

Betty Carrington: Betty founded the Blueridge Bear Initiative in 1998 and is currently BC Nature Director for North Shore Urban Bear Club. She writes:

> If you go down to the woods today . . . you'll find something good is happening for black bears. While black bears live throughout the province, the North Shore of the Lower Mainland has been one of the most challenging areas for managing human–bear interaction. Local governments, government agencies and bear groups work together to educate people, monitor bears and minimize attractants. A number of groups have taken on the tasks of overseeing fundraising, delivering bear-related education, attending bear sightings and attending community events across the North Shore. Groups include the North Shore Black Bear Working Group, Bear Society, Bear Network and Bear

Aware/Bear Society, whose coordinator Christine Miller and volunteers are the day-to-day workers in the field.[45]

Sandra Wilson: In 1994 Canadian Airlines was downsizing and Sandra Wilson was laid off from her job. The young wife and mother, wishing to spend more time with her eighteen-month-old son, Robert, saw this as an opportunity to start her own home-based business. For inspiration, she looked to her son's tiny feet.

Sandra handcrafted a pair of brightly coloured, soft-soled leather shoes for young Robert. Sandra then named the shoes after her son, and Robeez was born.[46]

Sandra began to wonder: if these shoes worked so well for Robert, perhaps other mothers would find them a good product for their children's developing feet. She decided to hand-stitch twenty pairs of her footwear and took them to the 1994 Vancouver Gift Show trade exhibition. The response was overwhelming—her basement

Top left: Betty Carrington, founder of the Blueridge Bear Initiative. Photo by *Cindy Goodman,* North Shore News, *4417*

Above: Black bear in a tree at the corner of Beaumont and Highlands. Photo by *Mike Wakefield,* North Shore News, *4075*

Left: Sandra Wilson, holding pairs of her Robeez Footwear booties. Photo by *Victor Aberdeen,* North Shore News, *4418*

Right: Don S. Williams. Courtesy Ken Fowler, 4463

Bottom: Blueridge Park sign, 2011. Courtesy Whitney Spearing, 4369

became Robeez Footwear's early headquarters and she immersed herself into learning all things leather, cutting, sewing, design, sales and distribution.

In September 2006 Robeez was acquired by the Stride Rite Corporation.

Don S. Williams: A Blueridge resident, Don Williams shared appetites for acting, media production and Liberal politics. In 1957 he began working in radio in Lloydminster, Saskatchewan, before shifting to television in Winnipeg in 1963. Through a link with the CBC hit program *The Beachcombers*, he relocated to the West Coast with his family in 1979. Williams gradually branched out as an actor himself and appeared in many shows before landing his ongoing role as The Elder alongside David Duchovny in *The X-Files* (1993-2002). Don especially loved working on *X-Files* location shoots in the Seymour forests. A self-described "raving moderate," Don ran for the District of North Vancouver (DNV) council several times.

Recreation

Four parks are located in the Blueridge neighbourhood. Canyon Creek Park greenbelt is the largest. It encompasses 10.18 ha (25 acres) west of Berkley Road between Rivergrove and Hyannis Place, with the Baden Powell Trail running along its entire length. Blueridge Park was established in 1974 and currently contains baseball diamonds, a soccer field and a children's playground. Byron Park consists of 0.49 ha (1 acre) east of Blueridge Elementary School and contains two tennis courts and a children's playground. Sechelt Park is the smallest park in Blueridge and is designated as a miniature park by the DNV. The Lower Seymour Conservation Reserve is also accessible from Blueridge through the Hyannis Connector trail, the entrance to which is off the west end of Hyannis Drive.

CHAPTER 8

Windsor Park

In the mid-1960s the District's new Land Department undertook a major land development project known as Windsor Park South, an extension of an earlier private development, Windsor Park. Windsor Park South was to be a step forward in neighbourhood design and the preservation of natural landscaping. The plan layout was done by Phil Hopkins of the Planning Department, a very talented design draftsman who was responsible for the layouts of most of the District's new curvilinear neighbourhoods of the 1960s in both the western and eastern halves of the municipality.

In order to avoid the clearing of all vegetation as seemed to occur in most private land developments, it was decided that the District would pre-clear the actual building sites on each lot prior to sale, but not

Windsor Park, 2009. Photo by Vickie Boughen, 3484

Windsor Park area; black outline defines Tsleil-Waututh Territory. Courtesy District of North Vancouver GIS Department, 3305

the front and rear yards. This decision gave future residents the opportunity to select which native trees and shrubs they would retain on their properties.

The entire Windsor Park South subdivision was put up for sale to a single developer in order to provide a certain level of continuity in the neighbourhood's housing. Engineered Homes was the successful bidder and although only five different house designs were offered, a wide range of coloured aluminum siding was used. This feature, together with the well-established natural landscaping on each lot, made Windsor Park South a very desirable place to live. When walking along Plymouth Drive a clear distinction can be seen between the old Windsor Park subdivision and the newer Windsor Park South subdivision with its underground wiring, coordinated housing design and extensive natural landscaping.

Schools

Windsor Secondary School: Windsor Secondary School was designed by Thorson and Thorson Architects and built by contractors Coyne and Ratcliff in 1960. The school opened its doors in 1961 at 931 Broadview Drive. The first principal at Windsor was Leon Lewis Dorais, a retired Second World War Air Force veteran. Since the school opened Windsor students have excelled in music, sports and the arts.

In the early days of 1974 musicals such as *Deadwood Dick*, a western melodrama, were performed at Windsor school in conjunction with a dinner. In more recent times Windsor students have performed *Anything Goes, The Music Man* and *Oklahoma!* at the Centennial Theatre on Lonsdale under the direction of choir and band directors Doug Irwin and Rob Carr.

Windsor is also well known for its excellent sports program. The school's senior football team, the Dukes, have won multiple Provincial AA championships. The junior team also took the provincial championship for the first time in school history in 2008. Gymnastics at Windsor are also well ranked, taking provincial championships in 2005–08.

In recent years the old Windsor school has seen many changes including the introduction of a French immersion program in 2009. The building itself has also undergone a complete renovation of the cafeteria and gymnasium, demolition of its "A" wing and portables and construction of a $1.8-million-dollar asphalt

Front entrance to Windsor Secondary School. *Ryan Crocker Photography, 2609*

running track around its existing football field. In 2011 the school celebrated its fiftieth anniversary with a multitude of events including the raffle of a 1961 Thunderbird coupe.

Recollections of School Life at Windsor

—by Eileen Smith

Windsor Secondary School opened in September 1961. The memories of that school year included such popular television shows as: *Car 54, Where Are You?*, *The Avengers*, *The Dick Van Dyke Show* and a version of American Bandstand, *Buddy Clyde's Dance Party*. Bob Fortune's squeaky chalk wrote our weather temperatures on his blackboard on

CBC's *Almanac.* We were listening to "Crying" by Roy Orbison, and "Runaround Sue" by Dion; lining up at the Cedar V to see "Blue Hawaii" by Elvis, and Bobby Curtola seemed to be performing regularly at shopping malls. It was the year Vancouver got its second television station CHAN and we danced the "Twist" at sock hops in the gym. John Diefenbaker was our prime minister and John F. Kennedy was the US president; the Soviets and the US were conducting nuclear testing during the ongoing Cold War.

In the years prior to Windsor opening, students from the Seymour area went to Hamilton or North Vancouver High School. During the school year while Windsor was being built, the Seymour area students were put on swing shift, going to classes for just a half day the first half of the year—some went to Sutherland. The second half of that year Argyle opened all shiny and new and all the students went there full-time along with the students of Lynn Valley.

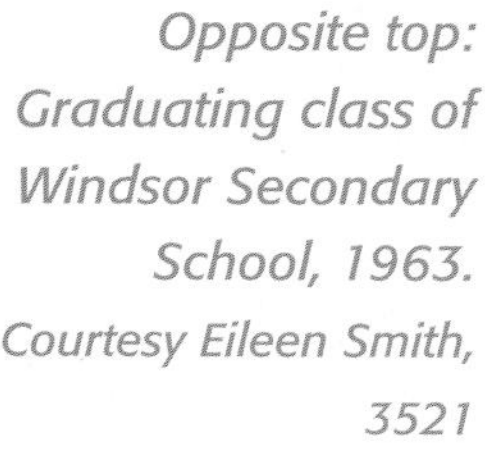

Opposite top: Graduating class of Windsor Secondary School, 1963. Courtesy Eileen Smith, 3521

Opposite bottom: Windsor cheerleaders, ca. 1970. Courtesy Valerie Spearing, 3415

Above: 1961 Thunderbird coupe, raffle car for Windsor's fiftieth anniversary in 2011. Photo by Whitney Spearing, 4452

Left: Windsor Secondary School sports club practicing in the school gymnasium, ca. 1965. Courtesy Wayne Smith, 1655

Right: Plymouth School class, division 5, 1993–94. *Courtesy Juli Hackman, 4118*

Bottom: Actress Sharon Taylor kickboxing, 2011. *Ryan Crocker Photography, 4658*

Plymouth Elementary School: Plymouth Elementary School is located at 919 Tollcross Road and was built in 1969 by the Johnson Brothers. During 1986 the school was used on weekends by the Presbyterian Church, with services led by Rev. Bernard Embree. Several generations of children attended the school before it was identified as a candidate for school closure as part of the North Vancouver School District 44 2009–10 budget.[47] The Plymouth Elementary School PAC and local residents formed the Save Plymouth School Committee in response to this proposal. The committee continued to lobby to keep Plymouth's doors open, but ultimately they were unsuccessful and the school was closed on June 30, 2010.

People

Sharon Taylor: Sharon is an actress who has had recurring roles as Amanda Banks in *Stargate: Atlantis*, as the kryptonian Faora on *Smallville* and as the evil Empress Amara in the webseries *Riese*. She received her BFA from Simon Fraser University and has trained in martial arts for over ten years, earning her first-degree black belt in karate kickboxing.

Naomi Yamamoto: Naomi lived in the Windsor Park neighbourhood from 1970 to 2006 and attended Windsor School from 1974 to 1978. She was first elected to the BC legislature as the MLA for North Vancouver–Lonsdale in 2009. She currently holds the portfolio of Minister of Advanced Education.

As well, Naomi's successful business career as president of Tora Design Group and later as president of the North Vancouver Chamber of Commerce sees her today as Minister of State for Intergovernmental Relations.

Gary Zimmerman and the Mackay family: Gary was a very popular drama coach at Windsor School, known to the students as "Zimmy" during the 1980s and 1990s. Students were grief stricken after he passed away at a young age and the theatre was named Studio Z in his honour. Two of his pupils, Gerry and David Mackay, became professional actors and directors. Gerry is one of the founding members of Bard on the Beach and he and David regularly act in or direct Bard shows. David is also a playwright. They grew up in Windsor Park following in the footsteps of their father, Don Mackay who has a lengthy resume of film, television, voice and stage credits.

Recreation

There are two parks located in the Windsor Park neighbourhood. Strathaven Park encompasses 3.5 ha (8.7 acres), with a children's playground and forested area. Windsor Park, 1.5 ha (3.7 acres), includes a playground and fitness trails.[48]

Top left: MLA: Honourable Naomi Yamamoto. Courtesy Office of Naomi Yamamoto, 4461

Above: David, Don, Gerry and Peter Mackay. Courtesy Don Mackay, 4653

CHAPTER 9

Tsleil-Waututh Nation

The Deep Cove Heritage Society will not attempt to record the thousands of years of First Nations history in the Seymour area. That is their story. However, their story is an integral part of ours.

Today the Tsleil-Waututh Nation possess an extensive collection of irreplaceable archival material including written documents, archeological plans, environmental studies and representations of their culture and traditions, which are available to us all. Their recent book and film *The People of the Inlet* was shown to a full house of the wider community of Seymour in November 2010.

We invite you to read our first book, *Echoes Across the Inlet*, to familiarize yourself with the earlier years of the Tsleil-Waututh Nation and the legendary Chief Dan George.

Tsleil-Waututh are the People of the Inlet. Intrinsically linked to the lands and waters of their traditional territory, the Tsleil-Waututh are a Coast Salish people who speak the Down River dialect of the Halkomelem language. The traditional territory of the Tsleil-Waututh Nation encompasses an area that reached as far north as Mount Garibaldi, east to Coquitlam Lake, west to Gibsons and south to the forty-ninth parallel. Today many Tsleil-Waututh Nation members live on the Burrard Inlet #3 Reserve located between Maplewood Flats and Deep Cove on the north shore of Burrard Inlet.

Excerpt from "Our Tsleil-Waututh Nation Declaration"

We are the Tsleil-Waututh
First Nation,
The People of the Inlet
We have lived in and along our inlet
since
Time out of mind
We have been here since the Creator
Transformed the Wolf
Into that first
Tsleil-Waututh. And made
The wolf responsible
For this land.

Tsleil-Waututh Nation Chiefs

1953–63 Daniel (Dan) George
1963–65 Garreth Thomas
1965–83 John L. George
1983–87 Richard George
1987–89 Richard D. George
1989–2001 Leonard George
2001–03 Leah George-Wilson
2003–05 Maureen Thomas
2005–09 Leah George-Wilson
2009–present Justin George

Opposite: Tsleil-Waututh map of traditional territory. Courtesy Tsleil-Waututh Nation, 4413

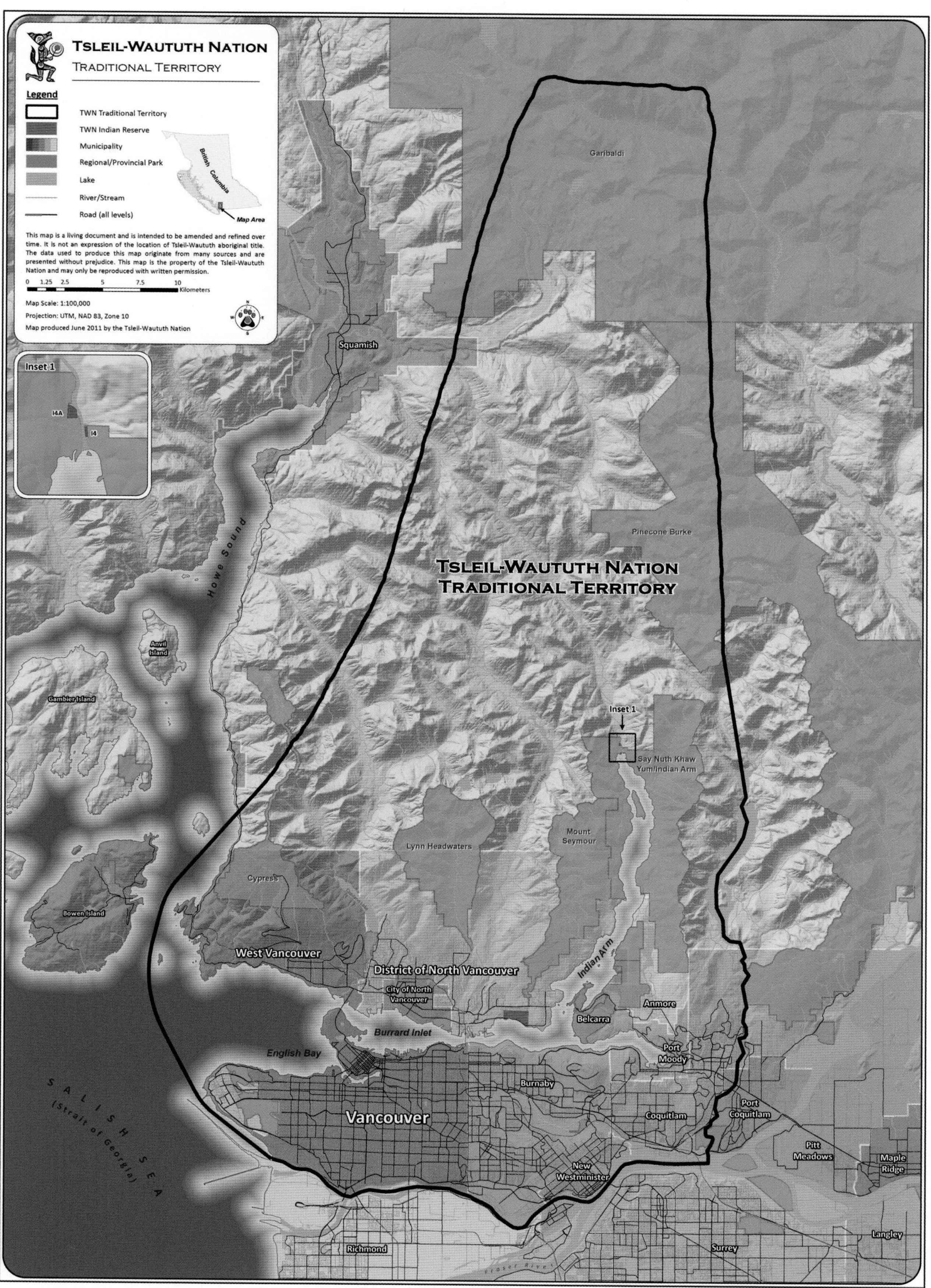
TSLEIL-WAUTUTH NATION
TRADITIONAL TERRITORY
Legend
TWN Traditional Territory
TWN Indian Reserve
Municipality
Regional/Provincial Park
Lake
River/Stream
Road (all levels)
British Columbia
Map Area
This map is a living document and is intended to be amended and refined over time. It is not an expression of the location of Tsleil-Waututh aboriginal title. The data used to produce this map originate from many sources and are presented without prejudice. This map is the property of the Tsleil-Waututh Nation and may only be reproduced with written permission.
0 1.25 2.5 5 7.5 10 Kilometers
Map Scale: 1:100,000
Projection: UTM, NAD 83, Zone 10
Map produced June 2011 by the Tsleil-Waututh Nation
Inset 1
I4A
I4
Garibaldi
Squamish
Pinecone Burke
Tsleil-Waututh Nation Traditional Territory
Howe Sound
Anvil Island
Gambier Island
Inset 1
Say Nuth Khaw Yum/Indian Arm
Mount Seymour
Lynn Headwaters
Cypress
Bowen Island
West Vancouver
District of North Vancouver
City of North Vancouver
Indian Arm
Anmore
Belcarra
Burrard Inlet
English Bay
Port Moody
Burnaby
SALISH SEA (Strait of Georgia)
Vancouver
Coquitlam
Port Coquitlam
Pitt Meadows
Maple Ridge
New Westminister
Richmond
Surrey
Langley
Fraser River

Takaya, the Tsleil-Waututh Nation wolf crest. Courtesy Tsleil-Waututh Nation, 4036

"Lament for Confederation"

Delivered by Chief Dan George at the City of Vancouver's celebration of the Canadian Centennial, Empire Stadium, 1967.

> How long have I known you, Oh Canada? A hundred years? Yes, a hundred years. And many many *see-lanum* more. And today, when you celebrate your hundred years, Oh Canada, I am sad for all the Indian people throughout the land.
>
> For I have known you when your forests were mine; when they gave me my meat and my clothing. I have known you in your streams and rivers where your fish flashed and danced in the sun, where the waters said come, come and eat of my abundance. I have known you in the freedom of your winds. And my spirit, like the winds, once roamed your good lands.
>
> But in the long hundred years since the white man came, I have seen my freedom disappear like the salmon going mysteriously out to sea. The white man's strange customs which I could not understand pressed down upon me until I could no longer breathe.
>
> When I fought to protect my land and my home, I was called a savage. When I neither understood nor welcomed this way of life, I was called lazy. When I tried to rule my people, I was stripped of my authority.
>
> My nation was ignored in your history textbooks—they were little more important in the history of Canada than the buffalo that ranged the plains. I was ridiculed in your plays and motion pictures, and when I drank your fire-water, I got drunk—very, very drunk. And I forgot.
>
> Oh Canada, how can I celebrate with you this Centenary, this hundred years? Shall I thank you for the reserves that are left to me of my beautiful forests? For the canned fish of my rivers? For the loss of my pride and authority, even among my own people? For the lack of my will to fight back? No! I must forget what's past and gone.
>
> Oh God in Heaven! Give me back the courage of the olden Chiefs. Let me wrestle with my surroundings.

Let me again, as in the days of old, dominate my environment. Let me humbly accept this new culture and through it rise up and go on.

Oh God! Like the Thunderbird of old I shall rise again out of the sea; I shall grab the instruments of the white man's success—his education, his skills, and with these new tools I shall build my race into the proudest segment of your society.

Before I follow the great Chiefs who have gone before us, Oh Canada, I shall see these things come to pass. I shall see our young braves and our chiefs sitting in the houses of law and government, ruling and being ruled by the knowledge and freedoms of our great land.

So shall we shatter the barriers of our isolation. So shall the next hundred years be the greatest in the proud history of our tribes and nations.

Chief Leonard George

Leonard George, a very remarkable man, is responsible for moving his people into the twenty-first century. His persistence and energy was instrumental to the development of their land and he maintains deep spiritual beliefs. He continues to hold an important role as a major participant in the treaty process. Of his people, Leonard says, "We were left behind in time and my main drive all my life has been, as an Indian you are never free in your heart and mind unless you cut the ties from the Department of Indian Affairs. My father Chief Dan George and my grandfather never dreamed that everything could turn around in our time and recognize First Nations rights."

CHRONOLOGY—TSLEIL-WAUTUTH

1700s Upwards of 10,000 Tsleil-Wautt occupy their traditional lands

A "plague" kills the majority of the Tsleil-Waututh people

1792 First contact with transient European explorers

1827 Hudson's Bay Company establishes Fort Langley near the southeastern border of the Tsleil-Waututh Nation

1850s The Tsleil-Waututh Nation move from Belcarra to the present site of the north shore of Burrard Inlet

1869 Burrard Inlet #3, Inlailawatash #4 and Inlailawatash #4A reserves created by Governor Douglas

1873 Tsleil-Wautt leaders formally petition Queen Victoria for land rights

1876 Indian Act passed by Canada

1880s Indian Reserves imposed by Canada

1884 The practice of potlatching is outlawed. The law would not be repealed until 1951

1927 Sale of Inlailawatash IR #4

1982 Constitution of Canada signed, recognizing and guaranteeing Aboriginal rights

1994 Tripartite Treaty negotiations begin with Canada and British Columbia

1997 Supreme Court of Canada rules on the Delgamuukw case, deciding that Aboriginal title is not just related to activities performed on the land, such as hunting or fishing, but to the land itself

2004 Supreme Court of Canada hands down a decision in the Haida Taku case that government has a duty to consult and possibly accommodate aboriginal interests even where title has not been proven

Above: Leonard and Susan George on the occasion of Leonard's sixtieth birthday, August 18, 2006. Courtesy Leonard George, 2141

Top right: Artist Zac George, son of Len and Susan George and grandson of Chief Dan George. Courtesy Leonard George, 2142

Right: Mask carving by Zac George. Courtesy Leonard George, 2146

Far right: Bear carving by Zac George. Courtesy Leonard George, 2143

Art and Culture

From *The Best of Chief Dan George*

by Chief Dan George

Of all the teachings we receive
this one is the most important
Nothing belongs to you
of what there is,
of what you take,
you must share.

"The only thing the world really needs is for every child to grow up in happiness."

—Chief Dan George from
The Best of Chief Dan George

"Community"

from *Salish Poems*
by Wil to Write (Wil George)

With open hands,
we bring cedar to the fire,
flame, and smoke.
We sing, pray
and are learning
that community stands
strong and determined.
Community is vibrant and vital.
Community is an ancient rhythm.

Above: Larry Jack carving, 15" tall by 10" wide. 4202

Left: Poet Wil George (Wil to Write) with a painting of his grandfather, Dan George, 2010. Courtesy Wil George, 4037

Right: Artists Richard de la Mare and Artie George in their shop, September 2008. 1067

Below: Chief Dan George and sons performing traditional dancing, 1952. Courtesy Mrs. Bob George, 0695

Left: Cates Park Protocol signing, DNV Mayor Richard Walton, Chief Leah George-Wilson, MP Don Bell, 2007. Courtesy Tsleil-Waututh Nation, 4775

Below: Performances by The Children of Takaya are popular with the whole community, Cates Park, 2006. Courtesy Tsleil-Waututh Nation, 4481

Housing and Development

In 1989–90 Chief Leonard George began consultations with Tseil-Waututh community members that led to the development of certain areas of Tsleil-Waututh reserve lands into high-end affordable housing options for Seymour area residents. He found a knowledgeable and experienced partner in Loong Keng Lim.

Leonard was anxious to learn everything, from economic development and financing to real estate and design. Loong shared all of this with him and together, the Tsleil-Waututh Nation, Kuok Group and Native Strategic Investments formed a partnership called TAKaya Developments. TAKaya Developments is now a successful real estate development company, majority owned by the Tsleil-Waututh Nation.

TAKaya Developments immediately went forward with building Raven Woods housing development, which currently comprises 847 homes. As with all development of this magnitude there were many hurdles to overcome, from the District of

Top: Raven Woods development, 2009. Photo by Vickie Boughen, 2681

Middle left: Tsleil-Waututh Community Centre. Courtesy Tsleil-Waututh Nation, 4487

Middle right: Tsleil-Waututh Community Centre during the premiere screening of People of the Inlet*, November 2010. 4148*

Bottom, left to right: Loong Keng Lim, Robert Kuok, Leonard George and Matthew Thomas. Courtesy Tsleil-Waututh Nation, 4108

Opposite top: Tsleil-Waututh War Canoe in Indian Arm. Courtesy Tsleil-Waututh Nation, 4483

North Vancouver building compliance to local residents who did not welcome the additional population or the intrusion onto the wooded slopes of the First Nations property.

However, the completed strata-style condominiums proved to be an attractive and well-received addition to the Seymour area. Raven Woods offers affordable housing alternatives for seniors and young homeowners alike, making it possible for them to live in the Seymour area.

Above: Burrard Band War Canoe racing team, ca. 1946. Top row, left to right: John L. George, Frank Thomas, Leslie Thomas, Andrew Jack (suit), Robert (Bob) George Sr., Ernie George, Dan George, Herbert (Paddy) George. Bottom row, left to right: Dennis (Denny) Thomas, Bill Thomas, Larry Jack, Ignatius Sunrays (Genne) George.
Courtesy Mrs. Bob George, 0698

Recreation and Community Facilities

Takaya Driving Range: Takaya Golf Centre is located near both Northlands and Seymour golf courses, at the bottom of Apex Avenue. The 270-yard driving range has been voted in North America's top one hundred golf ranges on four separate occasions. It offers seventy-eight stalls, night golfing, practice pitching/putting, mini-putt course and full service lounge available for public use.

Tsleil-Waututh Community Centre: The Tsleil-Waututh Community Centre is located in the heart of the Tsleil-Waututh community. It offers a full gymnasium and facilities that provide space for sporting events and community gatherings. The centre is also accessible for rental by non-Tsleil-Waututh individuals, groups and organizations.

Tsleil-Waututh Nation Skills Development Centre: The Tsleil-Waututh Nation Skills Development Centre offers employment and training in human resources, professional development, K-12 educational courses, counselling and remediation.

Tsleil-Waututh Child and Family Development Centre: The Tsleil-Waututh Child and Family Development Centre works to promote healthy development in children, families and the community by using a strength-based approach that is family focused, community based and culturally inclusive.

Merchants

Burrard General Store: The Burrard General Store is located in the Tsleil-Waututh Nation community and sells a variety of food, drinks, convenience items and clothing.

Inlailawatash Forestry Limited Partnership (IFLP): Established in 2004, Inlailawatash Forestry Limited Partnership (IFLP) is an environmental consulting services provider whose operational conduct is guided by the vision and values of the Tsleil-Waututh Nation and whose mandate is to support the Nation's community development aspirations by increasing capacity through the training and employment of community members. Inlailawatash delivers services to First Nation and other government crown organizations and the private sector in a holistic approach that allows Inlailawatash to take into account the social and environmental values of the community in which the organization is based.

Environment

The Seymour area has always offered rich natural resources. First Nations people had a steady supply of fish, shellfish (including mussels, clams, oysters, shrimp and crabs) game, berries, herbs; indeed they chose well to settle in the area of plenty.

The ancestors said, "When the tide goes out, the table is set."

The First Nations cultures of British Columbia recognized the black bear in various ways.

First Nations peoples distinguished black bears from grizzly bears and through symbolic representations included them in their traditional ceremonies and mythology.

Bear meat was eaten fresh, or dried for the winter. Bear fat was used as a cosmetic and for mixing with pigments to make paint. The skins made up into robes, blankets and hats. Some First Nations continue to use black bears for sustenance purposes.

Infant Jesus of Prague Church

Adapted from a story by Mary and Pat Johnson

Seymour residents often pause when driving down the Dollarton Highway to gaze with awe at the small herd of deer nibbling at the apple tree and the grass at 3196 Dollarton Highway. They might also take a moment to view the small church and Marion Shrine that occupy this tranquil setting.

What they are looking at is the Infant Jesus of Prague Mission of St. Paul's Church. St. Paul's is the oldest church on the North Shore dedicated to serving the needs of Catholic First Nations people. The Oblate Order operates the parish, a group with a long history of missionary works in Canada. The current parish priest is Father John Brioux, who administers to the spiritual needs of both the Infant Jesus of Prague and the larger St. Paul's located in North Vancouver.

The original parish priest was Father Francis Quinland, who is remembered for his pious manner and demeanour. His successor, Father Paul Clark, is remembered for his "down-to-earth" attitude.

Father Clark supplied the impetus for building the church in 1951. Previously, masses on the reserve were held in a large home known as the Big House and attended by up to thirty members of the Band. The church construction was done by Band members with the help of some young men from the Squamish Nation and Father Paul.

The church and its pastoral setting exude what churches big or small are all about—a sense of peace.

John Pavlik tells his own Infant Jesus of Prague church story:

Infant Jesus of Prague Catholic Church on Tsleil-Waututh Reserve, 2011. 4094

The church was planned in 1948, the same year Czechoslovakia was taken over by the Communists. The Pope sent out a directive stating all newly built Catholic churches worldwide were to call themselves Infant Jesus of Prague, and the parishioners were to offer their prayers for the Czechs.

On my fiftieth birthday in 1980 we decided to attend Mass with our children at the church we passed daily but had never visited. At the Mass it was announced that Chief John George was going to the Vatican to be present at the canonization of an Indian girl.

When the Mass was over the priest and the chief stood in front of the church saying good-bye to the parishioners. I had worn a small Infant Jesus of Prague medallion since I left my birthplace of Czechoslovakia in 1947, and it was a surprise to find a church here with the same name.

Right: Dennis Thomas with Takaya wolf pelt during the Vancouver 2010 Winter Olympic Games opening ceremony. Courtesy Tsleil-Waututh Nation, 4425

> I took it from around my neck and presented it to the chief on behalf of the people of Prague as a thank you for the prayers of the parishioners.
>
> As I did, the priest took the medallion from the chief's hand and said, "I shall bless the medallion before the Pope."

Vancouver 2010 Olympic Winter Games

The Tsleil-Waututh Nation played an important role in the Vancouver 2010 Winter Olympic Games. They joined with the Lil'wat, Musqueam and Squamish people as host Nations to welcome the games to Vancouver and Whistler.

Dennis Thomas, a local Tsleil-Waututh band member, put his acting career on hold to become the Tsleil-Waututh community coordinator for the Vancouver 2010 Winter Olympics. On behalf of the Tsleil-Waututh Nation he welcomed the world to Vancouver on February 12, 2010, during the opening ceremonies.

Dennis has been featured on the APTN children's program *Tansi! Nehiyawetan*

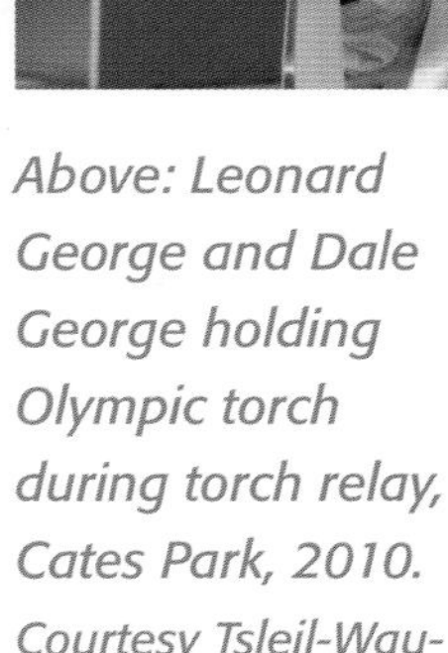

Above: Leonard George and Dale George holding Olympic torch during torch relay, Cates Park, 2010. Courtesy Tsleil-Waututh Nation, 4480

Right: Olympic torch arriving at Cates Park, 2010. Photo by Janine Coney, Deep Cove Crier, 4149

Chief Justin George making a speech at the Vancouver 2010 Winter Olympics opening ceremony. Courtesy Tsleil-Waututh Nation, 4485

(*Hello! Let's Speak Cree*) and at Storyeum. In 2011 he auditioned for *Wipeout Canada* while wearing the wolf pelt he had donned for the 2010 Olympics opening ceremony. He was chosen as a contestant and appeared on the show in spring 2011.

The Future

"We are looking forward, we are ready to meet the next millennium. The future of the Tsleil-Waututh Nation involves the fulfillment of our vision to maintain our sacred trust, honouring the commitment we have made to our traditional territory and to put the face of the Nation back on our traditional territory. We will continue to build capacity within our community and ensure that we participate fully on all levels—social, ecological, cultural, economic—on the decision-making processes that take place within our lands. In asserting our aboriginal rights and title, in working with partners who share common goals, and in being creative with our tools and resources, we believe we will come to a just conclusion to our 150-year quest to maintain sovereignty within our traditional territory."

—Chief Justin George. [49]

Chapter 10

McCartney Woods

McCartney Woods Neighbourhood Plan was approved on September 28, 1987, with the adoption by council of the necessary amendments to the zoning bylaw and the Seymour Official Community Plan (OCP).

McCartney Woods, named after early land surveyor and alderman A.E. McCartney, is a small neighbourhood located to the east of Blueridge with McCartney Creek as its eastern boundary. Access is obtained predominantly from Northlands Drive, which links Hyannis Drive with Mount Seymour Parkway.

The neighbourhood is too small to be fully self-contained and acts as a transition between the low-density detached housing in Blueridge and the medium-density housing in Parkgate. The zoning provides for a limited range of housing in McCartney Woods with conventional detached dwellings adjacent to existing housing flanked by smaller lots with low-density townhouses in the southeast corner of the neighbourhood near the intersection of the major roads. These townhouse developments appeal to the increasing numbers of older Blueridge/Seymour Heights

Right: Housing along Larkhall Crescent. 3092

Opposite: McCartney Woods neighbourhood. Courtesy District of North Vancouver GIS Department, 3307

households without children at home who wish to remain in the area but without the yard and other maintenance associated with detached housing.

Prior to neighbourhood design and layout a landscape reconnaissance was undertaken that provided basic information on geology, hydrology and vegetation. As a result the two arms of McCartney Creek dominate the design of the area. Also incorporated into the design are small areas of mixed coniferous and deciduous forest, some isolated cedars and an erratic deposited by the Vashon glacier some 15,000 to 25,000 years ago.

The neighbourhood includes a "tot lot" in the northwest corner with facilities for younger children and a major community park has been developed to the south providing much needed playing fields for Blueridge, Seymour Heights and Windsor Park, in addition to McCartney Woods.

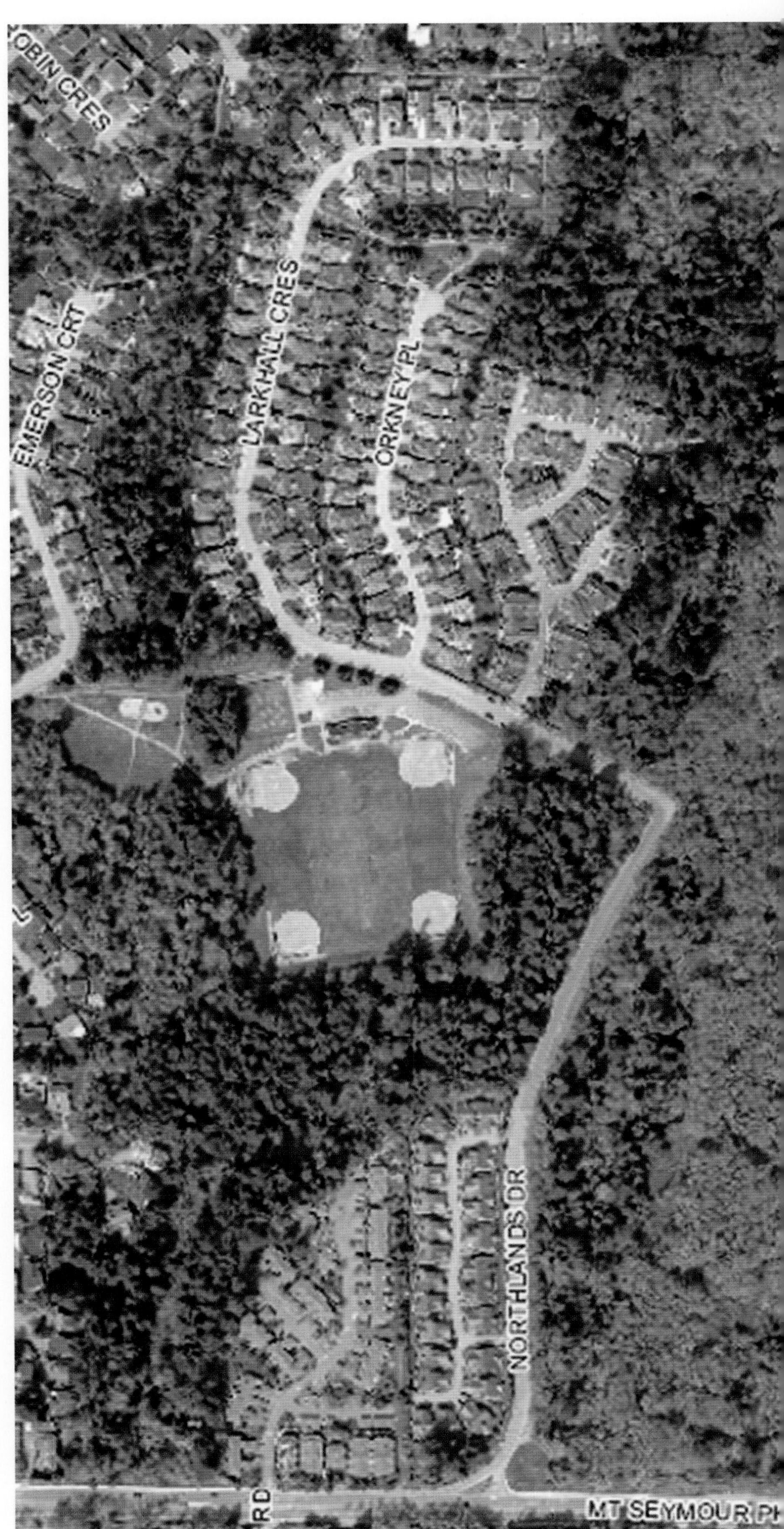

Recreation

McCartney Creek Park: McCartney Creek Park encompasses 18.34 ha (45 acres) south of Larkhall Crescent and West of Northlands Drive. Currently the park contains a fieldhouse with permanent concession stand, children's playground, soccer field, tennis courts and baseball diamonds.

With four baseball diamonds and accompanying facilities McCartney Creek Park is home to the North Shore Girls Fastpitch Association, a 2009 amalgamation of the North Vancouver Girls Softball Association and the West Vancouver Girls Softball Association, collectively active on the North Shore since 1950. In 2008 the North Van Pee Wee C team won the BC provincial championships, hosted in Summerland.

New snow on footbridge over McCartney Creek, 2008. Courtesy Lynda Barr, 2922

CHRONOLOGY—McCARTNEY CREEK

1982–86 Approximately 60,000 coho salmon eggs transplanted in McCartney Creek from the Capilano Fish Hatchery

1980s Windsor Secondary School operate a hatchery

1991–92 North Vancouver School District releases coho salmon in McCartney Creek

1997 Geographic information system (GIS) mapping completed by the District of North Vancouver (DNV)

1999–2000 Blueridge Community Association undertakes five major projects to enhance fish passage in McCartney Creek

Environment

McCartney Creek Watershed: The McCartney Creek Watershed originates in a forested section of Seymour Heights and flows down a steep incline to the Burrard Inlet, where it empties fresh water into the Maplewood Estuaries. The creek has four major tributary creeks: Blueridge, Mountain, Trillium and Woods. Urbanization, riparian removal, culverting and degradation of water quality have all contributed to the watershed's current endangered classification.

McCartney Marsh, one of the most productive and important marshes in all of the Burrard Inlet, has been devastated by poor development strategies, resulting in soil erosion and rapid runoff into McCartney Creek.

This is noteworthy because the Maplewood Mudflat is the only remaining estuary on the North Shore that has not been lost to development, and the cleanliness of McCartney Creek freshwater input is considered vital to the continued existence of the mudflats.

Chapter 11

Northlands

The proposed Northlands and Parkgate developments were planned to be the heart of a new complete community in the Seymour Official Community Plan (OCP). Both areas had suffered extensive forest destruction during typhoon Frieda in 1962, while the western portion had been cleared during the Second World War for the construction of the Department of National Defence Blair Rifle Range. The proposed two new developments were planned to extend from McCartney Creek on the west to the entrance to Mount Seymour Provincial Park on the east.

The proposed Northlands neighbourhood was designed by noted Vancouver architect Fritz de Vries in accordance with the environmental guidelines of the Seymour OCP. The design essentially called for a broad range of housing types suitable for different age groups and income levels. A key

Soldiers at the Blair Rifle Range, 1940. Courtesy Janet Pavlik, 0219

Soldiers and tents at the Blair Rifle Range, 1940. Courtesy Janet Pavlik, 0222

feature of the design called for a greenway of parks, sports fields, playgrounds and school lands extending from McCartney Creek to Mount Seymour Road.

Blair Rifle Range: The Blair Rifle Range is a large tract of land in the Northlands area named after Lieutenant Colonel R.M. Blair, VD (1876–1967). In 1905 Blair joined the 72nd regiment of the Seaforth Highlanders of Canada and spent the Second World War serving in Canada, England and France. In 1928 he was promoted to lieutenant colonel and received the Colonial Auxiliary Forces Long Service declaration. In 1929 he became the first ever to win both the King's Prize and Grand Aggregate titles at the Bisley rifle tournament in England. Shortly thereafter a large military reception was held in his honour at the Hotel Vancouver and the North Vancouver military grounds were renamed the Blair Rifle Range.[50]

Juanita Valentine recalls that a Mrs. Johnson used to chaperone groups of young ladies to dances at the Blair Rifle Range camp during the Second World War. They were picked up by truck from the Lonsdale Ferry and delivered to the camp for the festivities. On the way back, couples riding in the back of the truck would be separated only by umbrellas for privacy. Mrs. Johnson turned a blind eye to the goings-on.

The vacant land on the Blair Range, owned by the government of Canada, may be developed in the future if the Seymour OCP restriction on future development permits.

CHRONOLOGY—BLAIR RIFLE RANGE

1914 Target shooting becomes the first recorded activity on the Blair Rifle Range

1914–30 Land is used for varying purposes by non-military groups

1930s During the Depression the land is subdivided into 20-ha (50-acre) lots in a gridiron pattern
The lots are eventually reverted as the District of North Vancouver (DNV) fails to pay taxes owing on them

1940s Land passes from the DNV to the federal government to serve national defence purposes

Temporary camps are erected and training of troops commences during the Second World War

1969 Land sold to the Canada Mortgage and Housing Corporation (CMHC)

1971 The Boy Scouts and Girl Guides of Canada build the Baden Powell Trail through Northlands

1994 Approximately 70 ha (171.9 acres) of land to the east and south of Mountain Forest are rezoned to accommodate the construction of Northlands Golf Course

1995 Concerns over potential development of 2,150 new houses lead the DNV council to rezone most land to parks and recreation space. As a result CMHC chooses to develop only 710 units in Northlands

2010 Proposals are accepted for the development of the remaining rifle range land

Housing and Development

In the 1970s plans for the benchland at the Northlands site called for "Seymour, a City in the Suburbs," which would have created a city of roughly 70,000 people. There was great public opposition and the plans were later opposed by the Seymour Planning Association. Council abandoned the project.

Currently the Northlands area consists of detached homes along Taylor Creek Drive and Anne McDonald Way and several townhouse and condominium complexes in the surrounding area.

Housing development along Anne McDonald Way, 2009. 3099

Northlands, 2009.
Courtesy Vickie Boughen, 2668

CHRONOLOGY—NORTHLANDS HOUSING DEVELOPMENT

1989 McCartney Lane complex of sixty-six townhouses built at 2868–2984 Mount Seymour Parkway

1992 The Northlands, a fifty-unit gated townhouse community, begins construction at 1001 Northlands Drive. Expansion continues until 2002

1995 Strathaven, a 110-townhouse complex, is built at 1051–1196 Strathaven Drive

1996 Apartment building with 110 units built at 1144 Strathaven Drive as an extension to Strathaven complex

People

Kit Baker Family: Kit Baker (née Penny) came to live in a shack with her family in the wilderness of Northlands in 1928 as a four-year-old child. Even though the family was poor, her father raised chickens, had a cow and a horse, and cleared forest for a vegetable garden. The family was better off than many city folk during the Depression years. At the age of eight Kit was sent alone to England (by CP rail and steamship) to join her grandmother and returned three years later. Eventually she married her dentist husband, Fred Baker, and they gravitated back to Seymour to live in the Parkgate neighbourhood just down the road from Northlands.

Top left: Northlands condominiums' entrance gate and houses. Photo by Whitney Spearing, 4342

Above: Kit Penny with chickens, 1928. Courtesy Kit Baker, 0988

Left: Kit Penny and family feeding fawn, 1928. Courtesy Kit Baker, 0982

Recreation

Northlands Golf Course: Toward the late 1980s residents of Seymour started to lobby for a public golf course. The North Shore Public Golf Course Society (NSPGCS) was founded to promote the building of such a course and in 1989 was signing up members by the hundreds. In October 1989 over 300 people met in Windsor Secondary School gymnasium to discuss the proposal. The NSPGCS originally considered the Blair Rifle Range and other locations in the District as alternatives to the Northlands site. However, the rifle range was deemed too steep for a golf course and other sites were similarly unsuitable. And so, Northlands was chosen.

District council agreed to forego the sale value of about 68 ha (150 acres) of municipal lands and abandoned the idea of a new Northlands neighbourhood in favour of building the golf course.

The idea was not welcomed by all. In fact the Northlands proposal was met with scepticism by some. One prominent voice of opposition was Bill Blakely from the Deep Cove Community Association. The major point of contention? Whether

Northlands clubhouse, 2011.
4500

the DNV would profit or suffer a loss as a result of building the course. Dissidents believed that over $50 million in profit would be lost if the original 1988 District Plan was not followed. Those in favour countered that course revenue would offset building costs and bring in large returns. Regardless of this disagreement, course planning continued.

Six conceptual designs were submitted and the proposal by designer Les Furber eventually beat out the competition. Furber, of the firm Golf Design Services, also designed other BC golf courses such as Predator Ridge in the Okanagan.

Once the site and design were selected all that remained was to choose a name. Originally the course was to be named Northlands. Some thought it too similar to Surrey's Northview golf course, so the DNV advertised in local newspapers asking for public input. Granite Ridge, Heritage Falls and Ernie Crist Memorial Golf Course were some of the suggestions received. However, none of the public submissions were ever used and the course was named Northlands after all.

Northlands Golf Course eventually began construction and was partially complete in September 1996, when the front nine holes opened for public play. All eighteen holes were subsequently completed and the course had a grand opening in the spring of 1997 to much fanfare. The 6,504-yard, par-71 course was proclaimed by *Golf Digest* magazine (1999) as the runner-up best new course in North America. Northlands lives up to this reputation today and is truly a course "where nature is your playing partner."

Chapter 12

Parkgate

The Parkgate area had for many years been identified as a potential commercial centre to serve the more than a million visitors a year to British Columbia's busiest provincial park and the growing population of eastern Seymour.

The final design plan for Parkgate integrated a full range of commercial services, a municipal library, a municipal recreation and public health centre, a skateboard bowl, community park and playground, a church site and a variety of multi-family housing. The Parkgate long-term plan reserved land for a possible third secondary school and for adjacent playing fields. Most of the planned Parkgate development was built, except for a new secondary school. Parkgate is today considered a very attractive and functional neighbourhood.

Housing and Development

Housing and development in the Parkgate neighbourhood was designed to provide a variety of housing options including condos, townhouses, apartments and affordable housing for seniors.

Parkgate Shopping Centre and neighbourhood, 2009. Photo by Vickie Boughen, 2672

The Atrium entrance and apartments. 3931

Lions Terrace: Located at 1300 Parkgate Avenue, Lions Terrace was planned to be in keeping with mixed housing in the area. The low-cost housing is offered by the Mount Seymour Lions Housing Society. Opened in 1990, the complex has forty-five rental units of family housing with two, three or four bedrooms.

The Atrium: The Atrium is a fifty-four-unit cooperative housing project for seniors that exists only as a result of the efforts of a group of Mount Seymour United Church volunteers—Doris and Eric Bennett, Alan and Betty Hodgson and Ian Rathie—under the tireless leadership of Jim and Jean Roberts.

In 1990 Jim Roberts was named chair of a Mount Seymour United Church task force created to look into the needs of senior citizens in the area east of the Seymour River. It identified a need for reasonably affordable housing for seniors who no longer needed the space of the homes in which they raised their families, but who desired to continue living in the neighbourhood.

Parkgate Seniors Housing Association was formed, a non-profit society with no official relationship to the church. Columbia Housing Advisory Association helped the association secure a $25,000 loan as seed money to develop the project.[51]

Churches

Mount Seymour United Church: The neighbourhood of Parkgate can probably boast that it has two community centres, as Mount Seymour United Church was home to so many community groups well before we had the Parkgate Community

Leaving Sunday school, November 1959. Back row, left to right: Rev. Clugston, Carol Cantlon. Front row, left to right: Anne Wells, Jean Taylor, Sandi Booth. Deep Cove United Church building on Deep Cove Road is now My Little School.
4357

Centre. Today its acoustically marvellous interior hosts church services, concerts, choirs and memorial services, to name just a few of the many activities.

Mount Seymour United Church is a congregation of the United Church of Canada, which was formed by the union of the Methodist, Presbyterian and Congregational churches in 1925.

The present Mount Seymour United Church opened its doors on April 30, 1989. It was built by the congregations of Deep Cove United Church in Deep Cove and Mount Seymour United Church on Berkley Road, which had shared ministry since 1952.

In addition to the many church-related activities that take place in the building the space is well used by others from the community for public meetings, choir and band practices, music lessons, concerts and recitals, workshops and even recording sessions.

Church Volunteers: A hugely successful thrift shop is open every Thursday afternoon in the main reception area of the church that provides the Seymour area with bargains and an opportunity to recycle belongings. Unsold items are donated to charities such as First United Church, the Women's Crisis Centre, the Diabetes Association and several schools in low-income areas. The thrift shop was founded in 1960 by Gladys Johnston, who recently received the YWCA Women of Distinction Award. She organized the first garage sale in the basement of the church and the rest is history.

Donna Crook was organist and choir leader for thirty-four years prior to retiring in 2008. Betty Hogson was the church secretary during the late 1980s and 1990s and Brian Thorpe led the congregation in the new church facility until 1994.

Mount Seymour United Church and sign. 3914

Early on, Eric and Doris Bennett were long-term church council volunteers who gave countless hours of their time. Eric designed and completed the church glass window which hangs in the sanctuary.

On the first and third Monday morning of each month, church volunteers make sandwiches for the First United Mission in the Downtown Eastside of Vancouver and on the fourth Saturday evening of the month volunteers host a movie and fellowship night at the mission.

Mount Seymour Preschool: The church recognized a need in the community east of the Seymour River for a kindergarten (before it was a part of the school system) and began a private kindergarten from its location at the bottom of Berkley Road. In 1971 the school district added kindergarten to the elementary school mandate and Mount Seymour Preschool continued to provide early childhood education to three- and four-year olds.

In 1988 The Mount Seymour United Church Child Development Society was formed. It continues to operate Mount Seymour Preschool with a board of directors composed of parents whose children are registered in the preschool. A connection is maintained between the church and preschool parents who are also Mount Seymour United Church members. Since 1989 the preschool has been located in the spacious Parkgate Hall area of Mount Seymour United Church on Parkgate Avenue.

CHRONOLOGY—UNITED CHURCH

1937 First United church-goers met in Pete Cowan's Dance Hall in Deep Cove, served by student minister R.M. Warren

Doris Smith starts a Sunday school for the children

1943 Joint services are held in the Fire Hall (which became the Community Hall) with the Anglican Church

1951 Organ donated to church by John Moore, who had it shipped from Ocean Falls to Deep Cove

Dedication of the new United Church at 1890 Deep Cove Road by Rev. V. Vessey

Congregation has several "Work Bees"

Mr. J. Rawlings founds the church choir

1956 Deep Cove congregation part of a three-point charge with Seymour Heights and Lynmour

Men of the parish volunteer countless hours to improvements

1960 Norman Best tiles the basement at no charge

1960s Junior Forest Wardens under the leadership of Gus Muri meet in church hall

1963 Mr. Jongeneel donates topsoil and makes a garden; parking is completed

1967 Twenty-fifth anniversary celebrations

Junior church choir is formed

1976 Rev. John Sorocan retires

1980-84 Amalgamation of two United Church congregations; plans for a new church commence

1987–88 Sale of the two church properties make the Parkgate building possible

1989 New United Church at Parkgate officially opens[52]

Merchants

Parkgate Village Shopping Centre: If you say "Parkgate" most people will associate the name with the shopping centre, but it truly is its own neighbourhood.

Planning at the District of North Vancouver (DNV) had earmarked the area for development over fifty years ago, but it took until 1992 before the shopping centre opened.

Located at 3650–3680 Mount Seymour Parkway and 1115–1175 Mount Seymour Road, the centre developers were Parkgate Village Holdings Limited, United Properties Limited, the Bon Street Group and Canada Safeway.

Originally Safeway owned the corner lot on the parkway where a gas station was the first business to operate, but land swaps with the District finally settled Parkgate in its present location.

The centre is home to thirty-eight stores anchored by Safeway, Shoppers Drug Mart and North Shore Credit Union.

Fawcett Insurance: Fawcett Insurance has a long-standing history in the community. Starting in the 1930s Al and Violet McClintock operated McClintock Insurance Agencies in Deep Cove. Wilfred and Marjorie Fawcett purchased the business in 1970 and moved it to the Dollar Shopping Centre in 1974. In 1990 the business

Left: Parkgate Village Shopping Centre. 3911

Bottom: Parkgate Village merchants, 2009. Ryan Crocker Photography, 4058-33

moved to the Parkgate Village Centre and their son Jeff Fawcett and wife Cindy took over the company in 2000.

North Shore Credit Union: In the 1950s Joe Stump operated a dry cleaning business in Deep Cove. He was the only merchant who possessed a large safe (which apparently was left open a lot of the time). The North Shore Credit Union was interested: it approached Joe and started operating from the back of the shop. In 1977 the Credit Union moved to the Dollar Shopping Centre; it later moved to Mount Seymour Parkway and then to its present location at Parkgate Village in 2006.

Recreation

Parkgate Community Centre: The opening of the recreation centre in 1999 was a major milestone for the Seymour area. Parkgate Community Services jointly operates the Parkgate Community Centre with the North Vancouver Recreation Commission, both not-for-profit charitable organizations. Membership is open to everyone in the community. Working with the recreation commission enhances the services and activities provided through the community centre.

McClintock Insurance building on Gallant Avenue in Deep Cove. Courtesy Fawcett Insurance, 3962

Above: Groundbreaking for Parkgate Community Centre. Courtesy Peggy Cardno, 1010

Left: Parkgate Community Centre grand opening on September 25, 1999. Courtesy Parkgate Community Centre, 1452

CHRONOLOGY—DEEP COVE/DOLLARTON COMMUNITY PROGRAMS SOCIETY

1983 Deep Cove/Dollarton Community Programs Society registered as a not-for-profit society

1984 First Christmas craft fair at Seycove Community Centre

1994 First working agreement signed with North Vancouver Recreation Commission for services

1998 District council endorses a community management model for Parkgate Community Centre

1999 The 4,645-sq-m (50,000-sq-ft) Parkgate Community Centre officially opens. Partnership agreement signed between the society and the NVRC for the joint operation of the centre

2000 Construction of skateboard park

2001 BC Recreation and Parks Association Award for Facility Excellence

2002 Donner Foundation Award for Delivery of Alternative Education for Family Resource Centre Program

Website launched

Society begins to offer programs out of the Seymour Youth Centre

2003 Donner Foundation Award for Excellence in Delivery of Services to Seniors

2004 Emergency 911 forum resulting in province-wide changes to delivery of emergency response services

2006 Seymour Community Forum held in partnership with District council

2008 Twenty-fifth anniversary of Parkgate Community Services Society

Launch of Parkgate Community Legacy Endowment Fund by the society

The mission of Parkgate Community Services: To lead and empower our community to live life better.

Centre Programs

Parkgate Childcare Centre: The Centre offers programs for pre-schoolers six months of age to students twelve years of age (grade seven), plus before- and after-school care.

Youth Centre: The youth centre provides teen and pre-teen drop-in programs in its own comfortable facility within the community centre. A girls' group meets once a week and Smoovie Night Thursday is a popular event. Pre-teen dances for grade six and seven students can attract up to 500 youngsters.

Seniors Centre: Without the efforts of our valiant seniors in the community the Parkgate complex might never have been completed. The tireless lobbying of Mary Hunter, Peggy Cardno and many others who gave their time to working with the

Left: Parkgate Community Centre, 2011. 4576

Below: Construction of the skateboard bowl at Parkgate Centre. Courtesy Parkgate Community Centre, 1447

Right: Audrey Grisdale reads a book to her grandson, two-year-old Michael Boughan, at Family Place Daycare in 2002. Photo by Julie Iverson, North Shore News, *4261*

Bottom: In the Seniors Centre kitchen, from left to right: Peggy Cardno, Joanne Brook, Betty Edge, June Drake and Hazel Best. Courtesy Peggy Cardno, 1014

District was a great service to this area. For so many years the Old Age Pensioners had no permanent home and they were determined to do this right.

Today the welcoming seniors' facility by the centre's entrance offers a comfortable lounge, social activities rooms, and a full kitchen where lunches are offered on Mondays and Wednesdays. A daily schedule of events, outings and exercise classes is available. Special annual events include a Robbie Burns lunch and St. Patrick's, Valentine's and Christmas festivities.

The first seniors' coordinator at the centre was Dee Norris.

Other community facilities at the Centre include an arts and pottery studio, dance studio, gymnasium for basketball, volleyball and climbing, a weight room, youth skateboard park and a base upstairs for health care providers.

Parkgate Library: We have all heard of travelling libraries and our own library is no exception. The Parkgate Library certainly moved around a lot over the last fifty years. Elizabeth Austin, a librarian for twenty-five years who is only recently retired, says: "Long-time popular ladies

Above: Trixi Agrios and kids at Seycove Library, 1984. Photo *by Stuart Davis,* North Shore News, *4435*

Left: Barbara Alton, Helen Grahame Kaiser, Elizabeth Austin, Betty Crane, 1989. Courtesy *Seycove Library, 2981*

CHRONOLOGY—PARKGATE LIBRARY

1962 Although books were collected locally and exchanged long before the 1960s, the Deep Cove Library began in 1962 in a very informal manner. Geoff Mortimer the local druggist began collecting used books and 4,000 were donated by the community and stored in the back of the drugstore

1963 Concerned parents and citizens formed a committee to collect books and create a library

Deep Cove/Dollarton Library opened in the caretaker's kitchen of the Deep Cove Community Hall. There were 700 books and 150 members. All staff was volunteer

1964 Library was absorbed by the newly formed municipal library

1969 Larger premises were needed and a storefront located in the new apartment building on Gallant Avenue was rented. Circulation grew rapidly. Small story-time space allocated for children. Chief librarian was Enid Dearing

1979 Library expands and moves into the new Seycove Secondary School library. This compromise to combine a school library with a community library was an experiment of the 1970s

1989 Planning for a new community library starts

1993 The building in the Parkgate Civic Centre commences. The completed project was to include a pedestrian plaza linked by a walkway to the Parkgate Village Shopping Centre

1995 Official opening of Parkgate Library by Mayor Murray Dykeman and unveiling of plaque dedicated to Enid Dearing

2010 Library manager is Helen Grahame Kaiser[53]

at the circulation desk were Betty Crane and Barbara Alton. They pretty much ran the place, though first Noreen Ballantyne and then Helen Grahame Kaiser were the branch librarians in charge."

The North Vancouver District Library's Celebrating Our Community collection offers a selection of books by local Seymour writers, including Trevor Carolan, Bill Gaston and Shelley Hrdlitschka.

Library at Seycove School, ca. 1979.
Courtesy Seycove Library, 2970

Chapter 13

Parkway

Parkway Village neighbourhood was one of the last large-scale private land developments in Seymour. The land, located south of Parkgate Centre on Mount Seymour Parkway, had been assembled by the owners of Crest Realty over a number of years. Crest was a widely respected established developer of quality single-family homes in the District. This project was Crest's first venture into a mixed development that included single-family homes, townhouses, low-rise condominiums and a high-rise tower.

To meet the District's requirements for a new neighbourhood Crest commissioned one of the most respected names in Canadian urban planning, Harold Spence-Sales, a former McGill University professor, founder of the first university planning program in Canada and former head of the Lower Mainland Planning Board. Included in the design plan prepared by Spence-Sales were protected green space and lighted pedestrian walkways that led to a central park and playground. Two major north-south roads were required in the original design plan: Roche Point Drive, intended to provide an important traffic link between Seymour's major east-west routes Dollarton Highway and Mount Seymour Parkway; and Apex Avenue, linking Parkway Village to future development on the Tsleil-Waututh's Burrard Reserve.

Parkway neighbourhood, 1956. Courtesy District of North Vancouver, 2723

Parkway neighbourhood, 1992. *Courtesy District of North Vancouver, 2764*

On June 11, 1988, the District sponsored a community celebration day to honour the opening of Garibaldi Park in Parkway Village and the dedication of the Chuck Jorgensen fountain. Chuck was an active member of the Mount Seymour Lions Club and a District engineering inspector who supervised the construction of many new neighbourhoods in Seymour and other parts of the municipality. Mayor Marilyn Baker and a BC Parks mascot moose led the parade of residents and their children through the new Parkway Village neighbourhood accompanied by the Freddy Fuddpucker Band, (alumni of the North Vancouver Youth Band).

Housing and Development

The development of Parkway is a good example of mixed housing options that include condos, single-family homes, townhouse complexes, the Roche Point Towers apartments, low-cost subsidized housing and seniors' residential accommodation.

Pacific Arbour Seniors Housing: Pacific Arbour Retirement Communities currently owns two retirement homes in the Greater Vancouver area, the Summerhill, located in North Vancouver, and the Mulberry in Burnaby. Construction of Cedar Springs Retirement Residence commenced in 2011 with a planned opening in 2012.

Located on Mount Seymour Parkway opposite Parkgate Village Shopping Centre, it will be convenient for shopping, healthcare, the community centre, library, seniors' centre and churches. The eleven-storey building will offer rental accommodation of one- and two-bedroom unfurnished suites. The monthly fee will also include three meals a day, weekly housekeeping, transportation to shopping and appointments, and scheduled trips.[54]

Pacific Arbour supports Seymour community organizations and will provide a community meeting space.

Mayor Marilyn Baker opening the DNV's Garibaldi Park, 1988. Left to right: Ernie Crist (brown jacket), Mary Segal, Mayor Marilyn Baker, Mount Seymour Lions' Joe Thornley. *Photo by Mike Noble, 3120*

Roche Point Towers. 3895

Mount Seymour Lions Club: In 1966 a group of Deep Cove Kinsmen (a service organization for eighteen- to forty-year-olds) who had reached the ripe old age of forty, decided that they should charter a Lions club. Under the enthusiastic leadership of Joe Thornley the Mount Seymour Lions Club was born.

Top: Conceptual sketch of Pacific Arbour's new Cedar Springs Retirement Residence. 4136

Above: Cedar Springs, a Pacific Arbour Retirement Community under construction, 2011. 4507

Above right: Joe Thornley, 1920–2007. Courtesy Mount Seymour Lions, 2315

CHRONOLOGY—MOUNT SEYMOUR LIONS CLUB

1966 The Mount Seymour Lions Club was chartered on March 11 at the Coach House Hotel. Joe Thornley was the first president and truly dedicated his life to Lions Clubs International. The club chose its distinctive yellow-gold jackets and quickly became known as one the liveliest clubs in BC

1966–77 Community Day begins, which became the popular annual King Neptune's Karnival. Annual Easter egg hunts for the kids continue to this day, as does the Japanese youth exchange program and scholarships for the high schools. To the strains of "When the Saints Come Marching In" the club band entertains locals and fellow Lions at many conventions

Fundraising events include News Year's Eve, Bavarian Night, Hawaiian Night and dances. In 1975 Ron Morrice brings motorcycle races to the Agrodome at the PNE

Presidents during this time were Bob McClung, Don Allardice, Ron Morrice, Ron Dirk, Dudley Kill, Garey Ham, Ray Willox, Les Newson, Eric Bennett and John Lattin

1978–87 The club wins many District 19A club awards for Outstanding Club and Efficiency. It participates in Timmy's Telethon, builds a fitness track in Myrtle Park and purchases a food trailer. John Pavlik introduces Breakfast with Santa, which became an annual event

Mount Seymour Housing Society is formed in 1984, headed up by Garey Ham. Lions Court complex of sixty-seven units is built in 1985–86; Lions Plaza with twenty-seven units is opened in 1986–87

Presidents during this time were Walt Steininger, John Pavlik, Bud Marshall, Ed Cox, Kerry Baxter, Tom Lucas, Jack Mitchell, Bryan Martin, Bruce Loveset and Chuck Jorgensen

1988–99 Another complex, Lions Terrace, opens

A picnic shelter is built in Panorama Park and the club raises funds for and heads up a Youth Centre adjacent to Ron Andrews Pool

A pledge of $60,000 to be applied to a replacement theatre, which becomes the seed money for the Deep Cove Cultural Centre, is made to the Deep Cove Cultural Society. Lions Manor is built in 1988 on the site of the old community hall

Club members help build barns at Maplewood farm and with continued fundraising support the Man in Motion campaign with Rick Hanson. They take over the operation of Libby Lodge, a seniors' complex in Horseshoe Bay

Presidents during this time were Glen Muri, Colin Pew, Ernie Mayne, Rob Dalton, Don Plummer, Al Cummings, Bob Griffin, Al Bach, Bill Harborne, Tom Munro, Doug Clouda and Lou Destobel

2000–10 Raven Pub Night starts in 2002 and provides money for Christmas hampers, the Harvest Project and training a Seeing Eye dog. Club participates in the Shake the Can for Kids canvass, with proceeds to BC Lions Society for Children with Disabilities. Food services are provided for the Canada Day parade, Little League baseball, the bike festival, Parkgate Family Days and softball

A Lions community calendar is introduced

Presidents during this time were John Kusnir, Larry Chute, Gerry St. Laurent, Richard Stott, Jamie Innes, Geoffrey Wells, Al Cummings, Dennis Simpson and Dave Mair

Opposite bottom: Founders Park, 2008.
Courtesy Mount Seymour Lions, 2312

Right: Lions Club Band, Ray Willox and Dudley Kill, early 1970s. *Courtesy Mount Seymour Lions, 2341*

Bottom left: Trophy presenter with winning racer and Ron Morrice, 1976. *Courtesy Mount Seymour Lions, 2328*

Bottom right: John Pavlik presenting Bruce Coney of the Deep Cove Crier *with a Certificate of Appreciation in 1997. Courtesy Mount Seymour Lions, 2303*

The changes to social, economic and housing development by the Mount Seymour Lions has influenced overall change in the Seymour area more than that of any other local group. Their fifty years of service to the community is certainly worth recording.

The Mount Seymour Lions Club lives up to its motto: "We Serve."[55]

CHAPTER 14

Indian River

Named after the beautiful Indian River at the top of Indian Arm in Burrard Inlet, this 1980s neighbourhood adjacent to Mount Seymour Provincial Park was created under the direction of municipal planner Kai Kreuchen and municipal staff. At the time the radical new neighbourhood drew the attention of and recognition by the Canadian Institute of Planners *Plan Canada* magazine; the construction industry magazine *Canadian Builder*; the Globe '90 international conference on business and the environment; and the National Round Table on the Environment and the Economy.

The Indian River neighbourhood was designed in keeping with the Seymour Official Community Plan's (OCP) objectives

Indian River neighbourhood, 1963. Courtesy District of North Vancouver, 2747

Indian River neighbourhood, 1992. *Courtesy District of North Vancouver, 2769*

and based upon detailed environmental surveys only 80 ha (176 acres) out of 107 ha (235 acres) were developed. The first step in the subdivision design process was to set aside those areas that were considered too hazardous to build upon for various geotechnical reasons, such as slope stability. Once this was done the best natural areas were identified for conservation within the overall design layout.

Three large areas of prime forest were selected for retention in the final design based upon forest type (in this case Douglas fir forest with hemlock and cedar), the variety of other flora and value as wildlife habitat; aesthetic value; and the natural

Above and left: Parade for the opening of Indian River Park, 1987.
Photos by Mike Noble, 2385, 2383

area's chances of long-term survival close to residential development.

It was emphasized that these areas were not selected for traditional public park development but as true natural areas with limited footpath access connected to the neighbourhood pedestrian circulation system and the Mount Seymour Provincial Park trail system. A separate District of North Vancouver (DNV) neighbourhood park with grassed play areas, play equipment and tennis courts was provided next to the centrally located Dorothy Lynas Elementary School with its own sports field.

The remainder of the developable land was split up into district design parcels within the natural boundaries suggested by the terrain, soil conditions and hydrological patterns. In all, twenty-two separate design parcels were offered to the housing market at a variety of zoning densities, resulting in a wide range of housing choices. These included single-family residences, townhouses, apartments and even a high-rise, for a total of 1,290 dwelling units serving a broad range of income groups. Most of the development parcels were connected to transit, school and parkland by either sidewalks or lighted footpaths within the greenbelts that separated the parcels.

On June 13, 1987, Indian River Park was officially opened and the new residents were invited by mayor and council to meet their neighbours and enjoy a band concert, children's games, displays and presentations on how their neighbourhood had been created. The North Vancouver Youth Band led a parade through the new neighbourhood, followed by hundreds of children on decorated bicycles, to help celebrate the creation of a new and very special neighbourhood.

Schools

École Dorothy Lynas Elementary School: Built in 1989 Dorothy Lynas is one of two French immersion schools in the area. From its beginning the school had become the hub of the neighbourhood. The school was named after Dorothy Lynas, a North Vancouver school trustee who lived through the Great Depression in Saskatchewan in the 1940s. She held her post of trustee for thirty-one years and welcomed a high level of parent participation. She always held strong feelings for quality educational opportunities for all.

The current principal is Joan Martins and the student enrolment at time of writing was 566.[56]

St. Pius X Catholic School: The parish of St. Pius X had provided children with religious instruction for many years before their actual school started in 1996, with kindergarten and grade one held in two trailers at Holy Trinity Church on Lonsdale in North Vancouver.

The school building adjacent to the church hall at 1150 Mount Seymour Road was completed in 1997. A grade level was added each year until it reached grade seven. In 2011 the school had an enrolment of 260 students.

Churches

St. Pius X Catholic Church

Betty Hunter recalled a Sunday in the 1940s when Father Bader was saying Mass in the old Community Hall in Deep Cove. The hall was divided in two. Half of the hall was the church and the other side housed a very old, noisy fire engine. That Sunday in the middle of the service the si-

ren went off. Betty's husband, who was the volunteer fire chief, shot out the door and the rest of the congregation scrambled after him to see what was going on. When Father Bader turned around the place was empty. "It was quite laughable afterwards," Betty said.

Above: St. Pius X Church, 2010. 3867

Top left: The Pieta at St. Pius X Church, 2010. 3876

CHRONOLOGY—ST. PIUS X CHURCH

1930s Catholic parishioners meet at the home of Mrs. Stanfield-Jones on Caledonia with Father Corcoran

1940s Parishioners meet at the Community Hall in Deep Cove once a month

1950s Parishioners meet in hall behind the grocery store in Deep Cove. Father Beauregard instructs Pat Holmes to look for land for a church. Twenty-five acres are purchased at the corner of Mount Seymour Parkway and Mount Seymour Road. Decision is made to build a hall first

1961 Hall is built. Father Bader becomes first parish priest. Mass is held in the hall. Bingo and dances provide funds and social events

1981 Father Boniface sells a parcel of land, commences plans for a church. Father Neilsen proposes church design based on Pius X's local church in Bologna, Italy

1987 Father Pedro Lopez-Gallo (now Monsignor) becomes parish priest

1992 Knights of Columbus form

1995 Catholic Women's League forms

2005 A Korean mission affiliated with St. Andrew Kim Parish in Surrey is added to school

2007 Mission becomes St. Peter Yu Mission, serving the needs of Korean Catholics on the North Shore

2007 Gates of Heaven Columbarium, a repository for the ashes of departed parish members, is built, bringing back the tradition of the parish cemetery

Right: New Harbour View building on NE corner of Mount Seymour Parkway and Mount Seymour Road, 2010. 3736

Below: Sketch of Bemister's log home on Keith Road (now Mount Seymour Parkway). Illustration by Cranville of Seymour Series, courtesy Ken and Glenda Bemister, 0991

Bottom right: Cove Bikes' sign being moved prior to building demolition to make room for Harbour View building, 2009. 2596

Merchants

The corner of Mount Seymour Parkway and Mount Seymour Road has housed a few shops and services well before the shopping centre took over on the other side of the road. It was the last stop before skiers and hikers headed up the mountain. In winter they collected their coffee and in summer their ice cream.

Chapter 15

Roche Point

The Roche Point light off of Cates Park marks the point where the North Arm of Burrard Inlet, now commonly known as Indian Arm, joins the main body of the inlet. Roche Point first appeared on Admiralty charts in 1860, following a detailed 1859 hydrographic survey of Burrard Inlet by Captain George Richards of the Royal Navy aboard the survey ship HMS *Plumper*. In the troubled times following the War of 1812 and after US President James Polk's threat to take over all the Pacific coast up to Alaska, Britain realized that Burrard Inlet might be needed to provide defensive support to New Westminster, the capital of the

Roche Point neighbourhood, 1953. Courtesy District of North Vancouver, 2730

new Crown Colony of British Columbia, should it ever be attacked by the Americans. HMS *Plumper*'s survey provided soundings of Burrard Inlet and identified physical features important to the defence of the new harbour, lands that would be set aside as military reserves that still exist today.

The first major intrusion into the Seymour area by non-Natives came in 1885 when the Roche Point and Cove Cliff areas were logged off, followed by the McCartney Creek areas and an area above Deep Water (Deep Cove) in 1900. Minimal settlement existed in Seymour during the late 1880s, but the incorporation of the District Municipality of North Vancouver in 1891 and the subsequent building of Keith Road generated some weird and wonderful development proposals in the early 1900s.

In 1910 a massive private residential development was proposed for the lands south of Keith Road. Advertised at first as Rosslyn and shown extending west as far as Berkley, it was later downsized to go only as far west as the Burrard Reserve and renamed Roslyn. The site suffered from a total lack of services and it would have taken the best part of a day to reach Lonsdale by horse and carriage. This venture proved to be a total failure and the land was sold to the Red Fir Lumber Company, which proposed building a cedar mill and shipping its products to the Canadian Pacific Railway's terminal in Port Moody, via a railcar ferry.

Not to be outdone by other developers, in the same year the Imperial Car, Shipbuilding, and Drydock Company purchased 243 ha (600 acres) of land adjacent to the Red Fir Lumber Company for an industrial complex that proposed to employ thousands of people. The scheme was dependant on the construction of a railway bridge across Burrard Inlet at Second Narrows, or a bridge across the North Arm from Belcarra to a place in North Vancouver shown on the map as "Strathcona" (where Strathcona Park is today). It is interesting to note that the president of the Bank of Montreal, Donald Smith, whose bank provided funding for the construction of the Canadian Pacific Railway, was Lord Strathcona.

Captain J.H. Cates, well known in the early years of Vancouver for providing passenger service to popular local recreation areas of the day such as Bowen Island and tugboat services within Vancouver Harbour, acquired a large holding of land at Roche Point. The land was considered to have a definite industrial value and could also serve Cates in the future, if needed, to relocate Cates Towing facilities from leased land in the central harbour.

The District of North Vancouver (DNV) purchased most of the Cates family lands at Roche Point in 1951 for park use and the remainder was purchased during the 1990s. The District hired horticulturist Dirk Oostindie, one of the chief gardeners of Canadian Pacific Hotels, as parks superintendent, to design and build the new Cates Park, which soon became one of the most popular parks in Greater Vancouver. Dirk created an extensive system of District parks over the following years. Each of his major parks had its own distinctive entrance sign in West Coast Native art style, expressed in a carving created by Ken Oakes of the Parks Department. These signs became the hallmark of Dirk's well-beloved system of parks, large and small, along with his planting of thousands of tulip bulbs that bloomed District-wide each spring to announce the end of winter on the North Shore and pay tribute to the special role that Canada had had in the rescue of the Netherlands during the Second World War.

Whey-ah-Wichen

The Roche Point area, known to the Tsleil-Waututh First Nation as Whey-ah-Wichen (Faces the Wind), was used in prehistoric times as a seasonal settlement, apparently for a very long time judging by the great quantities of clamshells that were uncovered by an archeological survey of a midden in Cates Park during the 1970s.

On March 30, 2001, Mayor Don Bell representing the DNV and Chief Leonard George representing the Tsleil-Waututh Nation signed the Cates Park/Whey-ah-Wichen protocol.

The preamble of the protocol expresses the values that the stakeholders hold in common:

Above: Carved by John Ladd, inspired by First Nations' artwork. Courtesy John Ladd, 2399

Left: John Ladd (left) with Mayor Murray Dykeman. Courtesy John Ladd, 2402

Above: First Nations' totem in Whey-ah-Wichen (Cates Park).
Courtesy John Ladd, 2423

Top right: Detail of First Nations' totem in Whey-ah-Wichen (Cates Park).
Courtesy John Ladd, 2430

The Tsleil-Waututh First Nation (Tsleil-Waututh) and the District of North Vancouver (the District) are desirous of having an open and cooperative relationship with one another;

Cates Park/Whey-ah-Wichen is a place of aboriginal cultural and spiritual significance to the Tsleil-Waututh, cultural significance to the District, and a place of historical and recreational significance to both Parties;

The District and Tsleil-Waututh wish to protect and enhance the natural and cultural environment in Cates Park/Whey-ah-Wichen for the enjoyment of present and future generations;

The District and Tsleil-Waututh are respectful of their common and diverse interests and wish to cooperate with one another concerning the planning and management of Cates Park/Whey-ah-Wichen.[57]

Industry

McKenzie Barge & Marine: In 1922 John Kenneth McKenzie opened McKenzie Barge and Derrick Ltd. at the foot of Victoria Drive in Vancouver. Ten years later McKenzie Barge & Marine Ways opened at 3919 Dollarton Highway. Owned by Robert McKenzie, it is one of the oldest businesses still operating in the area. The shipbuilding and repair facility employs approximately twenty-five people.

Dollarton Shipyards: SS GM Venture *(in foreground) and SS* Arctic Ocean *in drydock. Photo by Whitney Spearing, 3164*

McKenzie Barge & Marine Ways Ltd., 2009. 3198

CHRONOLOGY—DOLLARTON SHIPYARDS

1920 Ichijuro "Phillip" Matsumoto comes to Prince Rupert from Nagasaki, Japan, to build wooden fishing boats

1941 He and his family are interned in the Kootenays during the Second World War

1945 Starts a boat business in Nelson, BC

1949 Founds Matsumoto Shipyards Ltd. in Dollarton

Pioneers construction of aluminum vessels

1978 Ichijuro dies and his son Sam and grandson Ken Matsumoto run the business

1988 Business is sold to Noble Towing

1995 Allied Shipbuilders rents the facility now known as Dollarton Shipyards

Matsumoto Shipyards, March 1982. Courtesy Rita Shimozawa, 1305

Housing and Development

In 1980 the Roche Point Neighbourhood Plan was adopted by council. The plan created a new neighbourhood east of Matsumoto Creek named Roche Point Heights by the Land Department, and a new arterial road called Roche Point Drive, intended to connect the expanding southeast portion of Seymour with the Parkgate Shopping Centre, library and recreation centre. This new arterial road connection to the Mount Seymour Parkway would have reduced automobile traffic on the two-lane Dollarton Highway, which was intended to revert to its original role as a "scenic drive servicing the Burrard Reserve and a small Dollarton community."

The municipal lands west of Matsumoto Creek were intended to provide a transition from the single-family densities of Dollarton to the multi-family densities expected to be built on the Burrard Reserve. When the Tsleil-Waututh started construction of their own residential development plan they asked the District council for permission to use the northern portion of Roche Point Drive in Parkway Village for access to their lands. This was refused as a result of negative input from new District residents in Parkway Village.

The Tsleil-Waututh were forced to clear the forested south cliff face of the Burrard Reserve and to construct a steep switchback road to the top of the cliff in order to build their new neighbourhood. Known as Raven Woods, this development has proven very successful on the North Shore real estate market. The western "transition portion" of the District's Roche Point Neighbourhood Plan to date was never completed, nor was Roche Point Drive allowed to fulfill its intended role in Seymour traffic planning.

Save Our Shores Again (SOSA): In the late 1980s Ramrod Developers put together a proposal to rezone and develop the Noble Towing/McKenzie Barge properties. The proposed Cates Landing project was set to rezone the properties from single-family

Roche Point Heights residences. Photo by Whitney Spearing, 3170

CHRONOLOGY—ROCHE POINT DEVELOPMENT

1500 BC Earliest known occupation of Whey-ah-Wichen by Tseil-Waututh Nation

1917 Dollar Mill established. Dollarton neighbourhood built for workers

1919 Cedarside Mill goes into operation. Only the burner remains in Little Cates Park today

1930 Dollarton Highway built

1950s Malcolm Lowry, world-famous writer, lives in waterfront shack

1957 Cates Park dedicated

1959 Land cleared for the park, grass fields, paths and boat launch

1969 The Pleasure Fair, a counter-cultural event with music, performances, artisans market and politics

1971 Village Faire

1989 First annual Under the Volcano festival

2001 North Vancouver District and Tsleil-Waututh Nation sign Cates Park/Whey-ah-Wichen protocol[58]

residential to medium/high-density residential and to construct eight large apartment buildings along the stretch of Dollarton Highway waterfront. In response, a group called SOSA was formed to lobby the DNV against the project.[59] The group claimed the development would impair the view of the waterfront from Dollarton Highway and cause traffic congestion and overcrowding in local schools. SOSA pleaded its case at a DNV public hearing on October 30, 1995, and the Cates Landing proposal was ultimately defeated by council.

People

Malcolm Lowry: The pristine waterfront of Roche Point attracted many writers and artists to this part of the world. The proximity to the city of Vancouver and living with nature were irresistible especially for those like Lowry, who was a remittance man from England and had no money or home. The prospect of living in a shack by the Burrard Inlet inspired him to write his masterpiece *Under the Volcano*. A waterfront trail in Cates Park named Lowry Walk follows the shoreline where Lowry lived.

Malcolm Lowry Walk cherry blossoms. Courtesy John Ladd, 2422

Kirk family outside squatters' shacks, Cates Park. Courtesy Jean Craig, 0444

See *Echoes Across the Inlet* and visit the Deep Cove Heritage Archives and UBC for extensive information on Malcolm Lowry.

Earle Birney: Long the Dean of Canadian poetry, Earle Birney founded the UBC School of Creative Writing and wrote many well-known works, including "David," a haunting poem that hinges on a profound existential dilemma. A friend of Malcolm Lowry, Birney kept a summer beach shack called Three Bells during the 1940s in front of what is now Little Cates Park at Dollarton. The poem "Pacific Door," his memorable plea for intercultural tolerance, was written here in 1947.

Dorothy Livesay: Celebrated feminist author and lifelong social activist, Dorothy Livesay twice won the Governor General's Award for Poetry while living on the North Shore. A friend of Earle Birney, she often borrowed a beach cottage at Dollarton near the Birneys', where she also befriended Malcolm Lowry.

Recreation

Cates Park: Cates Park occupies the major area of Roche Point and is of historical and recreational significance. Cates Park was named after John Cates and was dedicated in 1957.

Cates Park offers a wonderful recreational facility to locals and visitors alike. East Vancouver residents flock across the bridge on weekends and with the tempting odours from various barbecues and the variety of languages spoken it becomes a truly international place.

Park amenities include the Malcolm Lowry Walk, a children's playground, tennis courts, a beach with summer lifeguards, boat launch, Takaya Tours canoe and kayak rentals, a seasonal concession stand and a performance stage.

Environment

Roche Point Forest: Roche Point Forest is located south of Mount Seymour Golf and Country Club and north of Cates Park. In 1995 an environmental study revealed that the Roche Point forest was a unique habitat, home to the largest diversity of trees, plants and shrubs in any such small space in the Lower Mainland. Common animal species living or foraging off the lands in Roche Point Forest include deer, bear, coyote, eagles, owls and cutthroat trout.[60]

Two endangered species also thrive in old-growth stands of Douglas fir and western red cedar that the Roche Point Forest provides. The marbled murrelet, a small seabird from the Pacific Northwest, prefers nesting in the large trees of old-growth stands, while the Pacific water shrew inhabits the understorey. Living in long, narrow home ranges parallel to streams, it thrives on the extensive riparian tracks running through the Roche Point forest.[61]

Boy paddling a rowboat. Courtesy Susannah Howick, 3694

Right: King Neptune's Karnival. DHCS 2965

Bottom: Village Faire entrance, Cates Park, 1971. Courtesy Ray Eagle, 1169

Roche Point Eagle Colony: During the summer of 1987 Mary Huntington, the guider in charge of the Second Seymour Girl Guides, observed and photographed bald eagles nesting in Roche Point at the end of Dollar Road. Their massive nest, visible from the Second Narrows Bridge, was some 4 m (12 ft) in diameter and 2 m (6 ft) deep. The eagles' nesting tree was an ancient Douglas fir estimated to be between 400 and 500 years old, 2.3 m (7.5 ft) in circumference and 55 m (180 ft) tall. Ministry of Environment biologists claimed the nest could have been in use for up to sixty years prior to being discovered.[62] The nest was located on municipally owned lands that were slated for residential development as part of the Roche Point Land Development Project. So the Girl Guides set about lobbying the DNV council to agree to a 10-m (33-ft) buffer zone to protect the eagles' nest, if housing development was to occur in this area.[63]

The DNV eventually agreed to a 40-m (130-ft) buffer zone, and set aside three property lots, worth about $250,000, in order to give the eagles space.

Even though the eagles' nest survived the residential development of Roche Point some eagles were less fortunate. In February 2005 a mass culling of bald eagles occurred in the North Vancouver/ Squamish corridor.[64]

Bald Eagle. Photo by Damon Calderwood, 2934

CHAPTER 16

Dollarton

Seymour Golf Course/Roche Point/Cates Park, 1956. Courtesy District of North Vancouver, 2725

The dream of creating a "Pittsburgh of the North" at Roche Point fortunately faded and the land was put up for sale. In 1916, 40 ha (100 acres) of land was purchased by the Robert Dollar Company and in 1917 a large sawmill was built that would continue operations for the next twenty-five years. The company housing adjacent to the mill came to be known as Dollarton; however, the public school serving Dollarton–Cove Cliff and the greater area was known as Roche Point School.

Dollar Mill burner showing hillside. Courtesy John Ladd, 2373

Industry

The Dollarton neighbourhood was a thriving industrial site over fifty years ago and the story of Robert Dollar, the Vancouver Cedar Mills Ltd. and the Dollar Mill have been covered in *Echoes Across the Inlet*. The only remains today are the Cedar Mills beehive burner foundation in Little Cates Park.

Housing and Development

In 1944 the lands formerly owned by the Canadian Robert Dollar Company were sold to create a new Roslyn Park subdivision of large lots with easy pedestrian access to the waterfront. Sherwood Park subdivision followed next, infilling the area to the west of Dollarton Highway. The provincial highway had been built in the mid-1930s to encourage economic and residential growth in eastern Seymour. In the late 1960s the first municipal golf course, the Seymour Golf Course (leased to the local golf and country club), was rebuilt at public expense to improve the course and provide additional infill housing along Fairway Drive.

Sherwood Park Elementary School, grade 2, division 4, 1966–67. Courtesy John Ciacco, 3240

Schools

Dollarton Elementary: A school was built at Roche Point to accommodate the growing families who settled in the area to work at the mill as early as 1917. The school was moved several times over the years as the need for new premises became necessary. It was finally established at its present location as Sherwood Park School to service the Roche Point/Dollarton area. In the 1940s Burrard View School was built as a second elementary school in the Cove Cliff area.

Sherwood Park School: L'École Sherwood Park Elementary School at 4085 Dollar Road is close to the original site of the Roche Point School. Tucked in among the trees it retains its Seymour setting. Built in 1963 it presently has an enrolment of 387 students in kindergarten to grade seven.[65] Early principal John Kusnir (1979–89) guided the school through many changes. Before Dorothy Lynas School was built the population at Sherwood Park exceeded the numbers at Seycove and the playground was virtually a portable city.

The school introduced a French Immersion program in the '80s in which half the school is currently enrolled. The program is district-sponsored and students can continue on to Windsor Secondary School through to grade twelve. Instruction from kindergarten to grade two is in French only and students in grades three through seven receive 20 percent of their instruction in English.[66]

North Shore Child Care Centre has been operating from the lower level of Sherwood Park School for the last two

CHRONOLOGY—SCHOOLS

1917 Roche Point School built at southeast corner of Dollar Road and Dollarton Highway. Mrs. Olive Seddon Nye teaches at the school for thirteen years and travels by boat from Gore Avenue in Vancouver, boards with a local family for the week and returns home for the weekend

1923 A new one-room school built on the southwest side of Dollar Road and Fairway Drive

1926 Second room built to accommodate increased enrolment, now up to forty pupils

1933–39 Molly Nye (daughter of Olive) teaches at the Dollarton (Roche Point) School

1963 Sherwood Park School opens

years. Owned and operated by Natalie Whyte, the centre has between seventy-five and eighty children registered in pre-school and before- and after-school care.

Recreation

Seymour Golf & Country Club: A private company with shareholders Kent Grothers, Negus Grothers and Bert H. Lee was formed in 1952. They negotiated a lease with the District of North Vancouver (DNV) and in 1953 construction started on the corner of Keith Road (now Mount Seymour Parkway) and Mount Seymour Road. Clearing the land of giant trees was certainly controversial. The full course was officially opened in 1954 and Ernest Edgar-Brown, who became inducted into the BC Sports Hall of Fame in 2003, was the first golf pro. Following him Mel White became Head Golf Professional in 1957, a position he held until retirement in 1992.

The golf club was hit hard by Typhoon Frieda in 1962 and several hundred trees blew down, thus expediting clearing operations. By 1987, the new 1,672-sq-m (18,000-sq-ft) clubhouse opened and by 2003 the club boasted a total of nine golf professionals.

The golf course land is leased from the DNV and part of that lease requires the club be open to public play and to hold tournaments on Mondays and Fridays (excluding statutory holidays). The public is encouraged to use their restaurant and bar facilities.[67]

Seymour Golf & Country Club book cover. Courtesy Seymour Golf & Country Club, 2229

Merchants

The original merchants located on the 400 block of Dollarton Highway included Robert Stirrat and Percy Cummings. Information on these enterprising gentlemen who provided a grocery store and gas station to the early neighbourhood can be found in *Echoes Across the Inlet.*

Below: Dollarton Garage and gas station, 279 North Dollarton Highway, 1963. Courtesy North Shore Museum and Archives, 4724

Opposite: Dollar Shopping Centre with soccer team, 1962. Courtesy Rosemary Kenning, 1243

Dollarton Village Shopping Centre (*formerly Dollar Shopping Centre*): It wasn't until 1962 that the Seymour area had its own shopping centre. It was built across the road from the original Stirrat store by owner Butt Realty Limited. The Royal Bank of Canada became the north anchor shop and Shop Easy Supermarket became the south anchor shop.

An addition to the centre was built in 1974 by Standard Properties. The centre was renovated and renamed Dollarton Village Shopping Centre in 1992. In 2011 the shopping centre was owned by Anthem Properties.

Royal Bank of Canada: While the Dollar Shopping Centre was under construction the Royal Bank of Canada was open for business in a small cubbyhole office at 1012 Deep Cove Road. The manager at the time was Innes Mitchell and the teller was Alexander (Sandy) MacKay. Carolee Chute was hired as the first stenographer at Dollarton Branch when it first opened in 1962 and long-time local resident Vivienne Coverdale became head teller at Dollarton Branch from 1963 to 1968.

Supermarket Changes: Shop Easy Supermarket later became Stongs and then IGA. Sunday shopping was introduced in 1985. Stongs was taken over by Hearts, which was later taken over by SuperValu, which opened a specialty store featuring organic and natural foods. Today the supermarket

$ Dollar
SHOPPING
CENTRE
SUPER MARKET
BANK
MEDICAL
DRUG STORE
BAKERY

Above: Cars fill the parking lot of the newly opened Dollar Shopping Centre, February 1963. Courtesy Clara Bliss, 2037

Right: Dollarton Village merchants, 2009. Ryan Crocker Photography, 4057

is operated by Belich's Market under the SuperValu banner.

Government Liquor Store: The first liquor store in the Seymour area opened in 1974 at the Dollar Shopping Centre. In an area famous for its socializing, summer recreation and parties, it is hard to believe that until that time residents had to travel to Lynn Valley for the nearest liquor store.

People

Terry Tobin: Long-time Dollarton resident Terry Tobin began his education in the Deep Cove area at the Deep Cove Yacht Club, which served as an interim school during the Second World War.

Tobin was the first teacher hired at the Seycove Community School when it was nearing completion in 1979. He taught

science and had a lifelong love of the environment. His history of the environment of Indian Arm Inlet is available at the Deep Cove Heritage office.[68]

Ron and Pat Morrice: The Morrices recall coming to the area from downtown Vancouver in 1959 and purchasing a lot in the new Roslyn Park subdivision. Moving from a basement suite in Pat's mother's house with their three young children and building a home with a magnificent view was a dream come true. With very few stores close by they relied heavily on the home delivery of milk, eggs and bread. At that time the small grocery store on Strathcona would "run you a tab."

Ron used the family car to commute to work and the family did a lot of walking and biking. Ron and Pat are industrious, community-minded people and they quickly became involved in community activities. Ron became a charter member of the Mount Seymour Lions Club and Pat organized the first "Take A Break" exercise program subsidized by YWCA in her basement, for local mothers. After being led by the local "exercise lady," Shirley Macdonald, for two winters the program

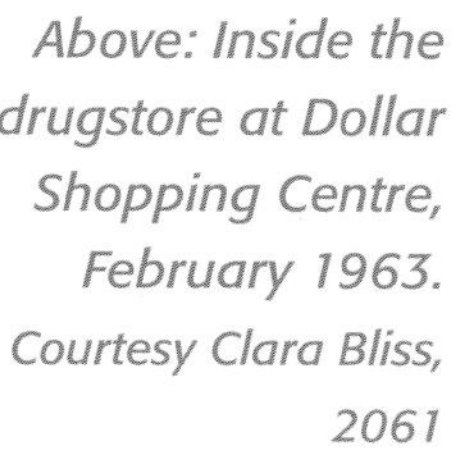
Above: Inside the drugstore at Dollar Shopping Centre, February 1963. Courtesy Clara Bliss, 2061

Left: Inside the newly opened Shop Easy grocery store at Dollar Shopping Centre, February 1963. Courtesy Clara Bliss, 2039

Bruce and Shirley Macdonald relax in the living room of their log home (pictured above), built in the 1950s. Courtesy Bruce and Shirley Macdonald, 3849, 3847

moved to the Deep Cove Community Hall where Vivienne Coverdale organized the ladies and child care. Pat has received the Volunteer of the Year Award and been recognized for her tireless efforts with a long list of commitments including the Heritage Society Garden, preschools and the United Church.

Bruce & Shirley Macdonald: It was always a dream for Bruce Macdonald to own a "real log cabin." On arriving in BC from Ontario in 1953 he and his wife Shirley set about finding a lot on which to build their dream home. It was to be on the corner of Keith Road (now Mount Seymour Parkway) and Dollarton Highway.

After an extensive search for suitable logs that even took them up Indian Arm Inlet, they finally connected with Paddy and Ernie George from the local Indian reserve. The Georges were experienced loggers who showed Bruce and Shirley how to build the home. After Paddy and Bruce had the walls underway, Bruce and Shirley took over. The landmark home is a lasting tribute to the pioneering spirit of Bruce and Shirley Macdonald.

CHAPTER 17

Cove Cliff/Strathcona

The Cove Cliff and Deep Cove neighbourhoods are often linked together in people's mind (and the census) because of their shared services and amenities. In fact, each has a character of its own. Deep Cove has a variety of cultural organizations, shops and restaurants; Cove Cliff has a pub, a hardware store, veterinary clinic, and automobile service. Deep Cove has a marina, a federal government wharf,

Cove Cliff area, 1953. Courtesy District of North Vancouver, 2786

Cove Cliff/Strathcona area, 1971. Courtesy District of North Vancouver, 2754

a yacht club and a municipally owned small boat rental facility; Cove Cliff has a municipally owned wharf on Strathcona Road and a small park on the waterfront acquired as part of the 1972 Parks Acquisition bylaw.

An early map proposed a railway crossing across Indian Arm linking Belcarra with Strathcona to give the Canadian Pacific Railway access to the North Shore of Burrard Inlet. Fortunately this proved totally impractical.

Cove Cliff is a difficult area to develop with a very rugged topography of steep grades culminating at its highest point with the forested Wickenden Park. A proposal by the Parks Department to add to Wickenden Park the land now occupied by Cardinal Crescent and Naomi Place, offering beautiful views up and down Indian Arm, was unfortunately turned down, as it would have been an outstanding addition to the scenic assets of the Vancouver region.

Housing and Development

Houses in the Cove Cliff neighbourhood came slowly, with prices for early lots going for as little as $50 on the lower end of Cove Cliff Road in the 1940s. Still affordable in

Cove Cliff area, 2009. Photo by Vickie Boughen, 2706

1970 and only a short walk down the hill to the beaches in Deep Cove, the Pavlik family chose to purchase their first home in the area on Cove Cliff Road.

Burrardview Housing Co-op: Located at 1475 Deep Cove Road, Burrardview Housing Co-op provides affordable housing in Cove Cliff. When Burrard View School was demolished in 1992 the Inner City Housing Society acquired the site and the complex was built by Progressive Homes Limited. In 1994 it won an Excellence of Design Award from the District of North Vancouver (DNV).

Indian Arm Dam: In 1965 the Vancouver Port Development Committee proposed that a study be undertaken to survey the flow patterns of tidal currents in Burrard Inlet, because of the development of the Vancouver Port. The primary reason for this study was to ascertain the feasibility of building a dam across Burrard Inlet from Cove Cliff to Belcarra Park. Damming Burrard Inlet was cited as having several upsides. Foremost, the tidal flow of water back down Indian Arm would have less force, allowing growth of marine industry along Burrard Inlet. The dam was also slated to be part of a highway and railway line. A rail spur was planned to continue from Port Moody, past Ioco, through a tunnel and over the dam to reach North Shore industries, bypassing the rickety Second Narrows crossing. The railway was to be twinned alongside a highway connector between the Port Mann freeway and Upper Levels Highway.[69]

Burrard View School and crossing guard. Courtesy Wayne Smith, 1640

Schools

Deep Cove Parent Participation Preschool (DCPPP): The DCPPP was formed in 1974. It originally occupied two temporary residences at the Deep Cove Community Hall and later at St. Simon's Anglican Church. In 1985 parents of the DCPPP organized the moving of a mobile to the grounds behind Seycove Secondary School. In 2002 a new larger building was constructed on the Seycove school grounds, next to the upper parking lot. A playground was added to this facility in 2004.[70]

Burrard View School 1948–90: The school played a major part in the area during its lifetime. It became an early community school offering many activities to residents who still did not have any facilities in the area.

It is difficult to record in this small space the influence the school had on the residents and the growth of the social fabric of this area over the years and we invite you to our archives to see the history of the school, many class photos through the years, and look through the meeting agendas of the Burrard View Association meetings, and Community School Education Programs. It is a trip down memory lane.

Cove Cliff Elementary School: In the 1980s there was much local controversy regarding the building of a new elementary school.[71] School District 44 decided

CHRONOLOGY—BURRARD VIEW SCHOOL

1940s Ethel Allardice and Parent Teacher Association petition for new school

1948 Official opening of Burrard View School by Commissioner Sowden and Chairman Dr. H.C. Graham. Within a couple of years extra space is needed—two new rooms are added

1945–60 A history of the school is available through the Deep Cove Heritage Society Archives

1974 Burrard View becomes a Community School

Bud Stymiest becomes Community Education coordinator

Information Centre is established and is affiliated with the Information Centres of Greater Vancouver. Clara Bliss and Barbara Old head it up

1970s Night school classes are popular. Belly dancing with Erica Ehlers shows seventy-five registered in 1975. Yoga, wine making and guitar classes were just a few of the programs offered. The Burrard View Association fights for a new secondary school and participates in the planning of Seycove Secondary School in 1974

1980s Focus on community events is still strong. May Day maypole dancing is revived, trails behind the school cleared by the Geddes, Kirks, Matthews, Callendar families and Trevor Agrios, Bobbie Grimard and Iris Fenwick are all out in force

Theatre, dances and lectures continue. Many courses were offered by talented parents in the community

1990 Old Burrard View School playground demolished before Cove Cliff Elementary School is built

Burrard View School with kids running, Tina (Smith) Langley with Shawn and Jonathan. Courtesy Wayne Smith, 1642

Burrard View School, Grade 1 class, April 1950. *Courtesy Eileen Smith, 2432*

CHRONOLOGY—COVE CLIFF ELEMENTARY SCHOOL

1975 Relocating Burrard View Elementary School to a new site in the Cove Cliff area comes under consideration for the first time

1978 On April 24 North Vancouver School Board trustees pass a motion to adopt in principle the proposed relocation

1978 Building an addition to Burrard View is suggested instead of proposed move

1980 Zoning bylaw amendment to build Cove Cliff Elementary School is shot down in a DNV council vote. It will take ten years of meetings before a new school is built

1990 Cove Cliff Elementary School finally opens its doors at 1818 Banbury Road

to close Burrard View and to relocate the school to a new site and building in the Cove Cliff area. A study by the DNV reveals that renovations to Burrard View were estimated at $1 million and acquiring the Cove Cliff site and building on it would cost $2.5 million.

Grand opening of the Cove Cliff Elementary School, September 1990. Courtesy Marilyn Myers, 1391

Seycove Secondary Community School: Seycove Secondary School was many years in the planning. Hard-working parents and volunteers in the community and members of the Parent Teacher Associations from both Sherwood Park and Burrard View elementary schools attended countless meetings. Seycove opened in 1979 with students in grades seven to nine. The first principal was Lorne Schemmer.

Parents began a tradition of providing money for scholarships and bursaries, with the Seymour Art Gallery and Deep Cove Heritage participating in the first fundraiser. The fundraising has steadily grown and today is supported by Cove Cliff, Sherwood Park and Dorothy Lynas Elementary schools. Thousands of dollars have been raised in the community over the last thirty years.

Principals:

1979–84 Lorne Schemmer

1985–86 Terry Shaw

1987–98 Larry Brown

1998–2007 Dick Burns

2007–08 John McGowan

2009–present Karim Hachiaf

The school boasts one of the best music programs in Canada. Achievements include Top Youth Choir in the World at the Kathaumixw International Choral Festival, first place at the Canadian National Choral Festival, Featured Chamber Choir at Carnegie Hall and twelve students in Provincial Honour Ensembles.

The Seycove Parent Council meeting on May 10, 1988, shows Jo Anne and Gary Salmon, Jim Davis, Candace Marshall,

Right: Seycove School ground-breaking, Mayor Don Bell (at left) turning soil, April 1978. Courtesy Lorne Schemmer, 1579

Below: Seycove Community School. Ryan Crocker Photography, 2615

Ingrid Deary, Cathy Martin, Larry Brown, Peter Border, Linda van Niekerk, Gladys Johnston, Sally Chamberlain, Sue Towne, Stan Joughin, Lynne and Earl Matheson and Sue Cohen in attendance.

Churches

St. Clare-in-the-Cove Anglican Church (*formerly St. Simon's Anglican Church*): Located on Deep Cove Road this picturesque country church has contributed to the quality of life in Seymour over the years, providing space for a kindergarten, thrift shop, socials, Sunday school, Brownies, Guides and Scouts.

CHRONOLOGY—ANGLICAN CHURCH

1940s Bertha Breedon writes: "There was no church. Anglicans, including the Rawlings family, met in a hall behind the grocery in the Cove. Eventually Mr. Naughton donated land on Deep Cove Road and the 'little blue church' was built completely on volunteer labour. Official opening was in 1949"

1972 Church is upgraded and much needed basement installed

1978–81 Rev. Bill Ferris responsible for building up the congregation

1987–2005 Rev. Ed Hird introduces a successful Youth Ministry and establishes a contemporary service in addition to the traditional Anglican Service

2005 Rev. Hird and many members of his congregation disagree with the Diocese of New Westminster's decision to approve same-sex marriage. They move to the old Maplewood School at 420 Seymour River Place for Sunday services and the congregation become members of the Anglican Coalition in Canada

2007 Church is given new name by the Anglican Diocese of New Westminster, "St. Clare-in-the-Cove." The new vicar is Rev. Carla McGhie. A labyrinth is added, and Friday coffee evenings[72]

2011 Building is put up for sale. Remaining congregation move to Mount Seymour United Church premises for twice-monthly services

St. Simon's Anglican Church. Courtesy Terry Tobin, 1732

Deep Cove Gospel Hall: After visits to Deep Cove from the Main Street Gospel Hall in Vancouver by David Jones and Bill Hague they decided in 1952 to start a Sunday school for children in the Deep Cove Community Hall.

Parishioners leaving Gospel Hall. Courtesy Wayne Smith, 1631

The Amble Inn Cafe, 1950s, was remodelled and enlarged several times to eventually become The Raven Pub. Courtesy John Moore, 0111

Merchants

The 1000-block of Deep Cove Road, on the southeast corner of Mount Seymour Parkway and Deep Cove Road, was developed as a small commercial location by Gus Muri in the 1940s. He built a restaurant, gas station and hardware store, and since that time many small businesses have been in operation there.

John Moore in his store. Courtesy John Moore, 0109

Gus's Hardware Store: Gus Muri opened Gus Hardware and Lumberyard, which continued to be operated by the Muri family for sixty-two years. The store eventually became part of the Home Hardware chain. In 2008 owner-operators Glen and Dennis Muri sold the business to Mike Tigges and the store became part of the Irly affiliate group. The store closed in 2011.

The Raven Pub: In 1946 Gus Muri opened the Amble Inn restaurant on Deep Cove Road. By 1968 an addition and living quarters had been added to the building. The name of the business was changed in the 1970s by the new owners, the Assimis, to the Spanish Inn. It finally became The Raven Pub in 1979. Ownership changed again in the 1990s to Del Feller, who opened an outdoor patio. In 2000 the business was purchased by the present owners, Jennifer and Peter Crawford. They advertise it as the Neighbourhood Gathering Place.

The Raven Pub offers express take-out and a cold beer and wine store. 4544

Other businesses that operated in the 1000-block of Deep Cove Road over the years include: Block Brothers Realty, John Davis Law Office and the Deep Cove Medical Centre, with doctors Donald Smith, Peter Richards, Rosemary Basson and Kay Sutherland.

Present-day Cove Cliff businesses include: Marion Culham's accounting office, which opened in 1983; Gus Muri's Texaco garage, which opened in the 1940s and became Central Motors in 1980 (owned and operated by Tony Jamashita); Deep Cove Music, opened in 1997

Alma Lima outside the Highway Market located next to the gas station at Mount Seymour Parkway south of Deep Cove Road, May 1960. Courtesy Butch Lima, 1294

Sid Speight at the Shell Service Station on Coronation Day, June 1953 (note the Union Jack flag). Courtesy Margaret B. Roberge, 4003

(owned and operated by Tyler Pearson); Musart, which is involved in Cates Park concerts and Deep Cove Daze; and Seymour Animal Clinic, operated by Dr. Brad Gilbert and Dr. June Milliken since 2001.

Gillis Homestead/Strathcona Store: The Gillis Homestead was built in 1926 at what is now 1207 Harris Avenue. The building became the Strathcona Store in 1936. From 1956–66 the store also housed the local post office.

Strathcona Store. Courtesy Terry Tobin, 1716

People

Don Allardice: Don lived in the Cove Cliff area for many years and is fondly remembered as one of the charter members of the Mount Seymour Lions Club. He also headed up the Lions Society for Children with Disabilites for a few years, supported new charter clubs on the North Shore and was a major proponent of building Lions affordable housing in the Seymour area. Founders Park in the Parkway neighbourhood is named after Don, as well as Ron Morrice and Joe Thornley.

Lori-Ann Speed: Lori-Ann has been playing piano since the age of eight. She earned her Bachelor of Music degree from UBC and then studied music and language at the University of Grenoble in France. Returning home she took part in an exclusive program studying composition and recording techniques for film. This venture led to soundtrack work for film and documentaries. In 1994 she shifted her focus to recording and performing her own compositions. She has seven albums to her credit including *In Search of Wings*, a top seller when it was released in 1994. *In the Wake of a Whisper* was recorded at UBC's Chan Centre for Performing Arts and nominated for Best Instrumental Album (non-classical) at the 2001 West Coast Music Awards.

Henry Young: Guitarist and Juno Award nominee Henry Young has lived in the Strathcona Drive area since 1978, while working internationally with fellow musicians of the highest renown. A former member of Nina Simone's superlative band, his performances at Carnegie Hall, the prestigious Montreux and Newport jazz festivals and elsewhere have won praise from Ray Charles, Miles Davis and Wes Montgomery. Young's talents as arranger, composer, musical director and accompanist have seen him work alongside B.B. King, Little Richard, Thelonious Monk, the Supremes and other stars. His album work includes *Looking Back, Cooking on Sunday, In Your Face* and Simone's unbeatable double-set *Live in Europe.*

Gus Muri: Although he and his family lived on Burns Avenue (now Panorama Drive), Gus had a huge influence on the development of Cove Cliff and the surrounding area. His entrepreneurial spirit came with him from Saskatchewan in the 1940s and his successful blacktop paving business flourished. He purchased land at the corner of Mount Seymour and Deep Cove Road and built a service station that originally offered Shell and then Texaco products.[73]

He then switched to operating a hardware and lumber supply store. His sons Glen and Dennis joined him in the business, Dennis originally with the paving business and Glen with bookkeeping for the hardware store. Granddaughter Lisa Muri is still very much involved in community affairs and has served on the DNV as a councillor for the last fifteen years.

Gillis' second home, The Homestead, on Harris Avenue. Courtesy Christena Gillis, 0609

Harvey Burt: In 1950 while looking for a weekend place at Dollarton, Harvey Burt, an English teacher, and his wife Dorothy met Malcolm Lowry and his wife Margerie Bonner, formally a Hollywood actress, and they became best friends. With his passion for literature and local heritage, Harvey became a frequent interview subject within the "Lowry Industry." After his friend's death their extensive correspondence was published in *Sursum Corda! The Collected Letters of Malcolm Lowry*, edited by Sherrill Grace. An eloquent Seymour gentleman, Harvey became a tireless advocate with the Deep Cove Heritage Society.

Right: Wickenden Park. 4077–07

Below: Wickenden Park steps to trail entrance. 4077–04

Below right: Myrtle Park sign. 4117

Recreation

Wickenden Park: Named after Reeve W.O. Wickenden, of North Vancouver, 1902.

Strathcona Park: A delightful jewel of a park located on the waterfront on Strathcona Road. The land was purchased by the DNV and is also accessible from the trail through Myrtle Park. Archeology students from Simon Fraser University, in collaboration with Tsleil-Waututh Nation, completed an excavation in August 2000. A valuable Native midden was discovered.

Myrtle Park: Myrtle Park was named after the small, brightly coloured American songbird with a weak, unmusical song. We are not sure who was responsible for naming the park or whether a myrtle was ever spotted here!

In the 1950s Omar Hanson and fellow Kinsman Bob Wells, who was always full of great ideas, dreamed up a scheme that the club should have a scenic railway in Myrtle Park, as a locomotive was available free on Vancouver Island. Needless to say the freight cost broke their bank accounts and their backs and the project was abandoned.

CHRONOLOGY—MYRTLE PARK

1950s The area of Myrtle Park already housed a dirt playing field

1960s The beginning of official development of Myrtle Park

1961 Development of a second playing field

1965–66 Tennis court developed

1965 Installation of Minor League backstop at the southeast corner of the all-weather field

1979 Myrtle Park field house is built, containing change rooms, showers and fixtures

1980 Additional playground equipment approved for east side of Myrtle Park, next to Strathcona Road

1988 Addition to the field house

2001 Old field house burns down

2002 The DNV passes the Myrtle Park Dedication bylaw, through referendum vote, to officially define the borders of Myrtle Park

2003 New Myrtle Park field house is built, containing showers, change rooms and concession stand

2011 Facilities in the park include baseball diamond, soccer field, tennis courts, children's playground, off-leash dog walk, waterpark, field house, lacrosse box and walking trails

Cove Cliff Country Club. Few people remember this small ranch located halfway up Cove Cliff Road.
Courtesy Terry Tobin, 1728

Environment

Grey Rocks Island: This picturesque island lies 183 m (200 yds) off the beach at the foot of Strathcona Road. In 1859 Captain Richards of HMS *Plumper* named it White Rock on his first survey of Burrard Inlet and Indian Arm. The Native name is Spuka-nah-ah and it has come to be known as Grey Rocks.

A 1947 document shows title to the land registered in the name of Annie M. Rand. By the 1950s the island here was a summer camp with three cabins. In the 1970s the DNV could have bought the Island for $85,000; however, mayor Ron Andrews and council turned it down. The cottage-style house on the island was built in 1993 and designed by Brian Bydwell Architect Ltd.[74]

Above: Walking trail around the perimeter of Myrtle Park in spring. 4475

Right: Grey Rocks Island at the foot of Strathcona. DCHS, 0047

Chapter 18

Deep Cove

For thousands of years Deep Cove was a very different place from what we see today. The primeval forest of giant trees—Douglas fir, western red cedar and Sitka spruce—dominated the slopes of Mount Seymour right down to the waters of the sea. Wild animals we rarely see now such as wolves, cougars and elk roamed the forest, ravines and open spaces. Pods of orcas regularly swam north to the mouth of Indian River at the head of the Arm in search of the huge runs of coho, chum and

Second Street, now Gallant Avenue, 1950s. Courtesy Jim Donald, 0002

Deep Cove, 2009. Photo by Vickie Boughen, 2715

pink salmon, as well as steelhead trout. In those early years one might have seen through the morning mists the long cedar canoes of the Tsleil-Waututh First Nation, the People of the Inlet, heading north to claim their share of the salmon harvest.

In 1792 the Spanish explored Indian Arm. It was almost a century before there was any significant activity in the Deep Water area, as Deep Cove was then called. Early development took the form of summer cottages for residents of Vancouver. During the Great Depression of the 1930s most of the summer cottages were converted to full-time residences as a convenient alternative to the more expensive housing elsewhere in Vancouver. By 1961 there were 402 people living in 148 dwelling units in Deep Cove.

A 1963 report to council by municipal planner Martin Chesworth recommended that the District undertake a municipal initiative in road construction, public parks and terraces, and encourage private action to revitalize the business section of Deep Cove. PARKS 63, a major park plan, and PLAN 64, a comprehensive master plan for the entire District, proposed many improvements to the Deep Cove neighbourhood.

In July 1983 council adopted the Deep Cove Official Community Plan (OCP), which led to a 1985 Panorama–Deep Cove Park Design Plan prepared by Diamond, Guzzi, Perry, Wuori Landscape Architects, under the direction of a Technical Advisory Committee headed by Dirk Oostindie, District of North Vancouver (DNV) Parks Superintendent. This long-range plan created the Deep Cove improvements we see today.

Housing and Development

As Deep Cove moved from a summer resort to permanent reasonable housing during the 1940s, values continued to gradually increase to the high prices of today.

Deep Cove has truly transitioned from cottage country to suburbia. And due to spectacular scenery, a village atmosphere and an easy drive from Vancouver, it is still a summertime hot spot on the North Shore.

Development in the Cove was inevitable with Vancouver growing so rapidly and building lots in this area were still cheaper than those in the city. The history of growth in the Cove over the last forty years has been an extremely painful process with countless battles with the District councils and local residents. Much controversy began with the arrival of the first apartment block in 1971 on the 400-block of Gallant Avenue, as it became clear that building codes and regulations were very lax or non-existent in those days.

Houses along Panorama Drive, 1970s. Photo by Adrian Schweitzer, 4579-20

Houseboats: Described as "Shanty Live-Aboards," the first of over forty illegally moored vessels of all shapes and sizes began to appear in the early 1970s. Local residents again rose up in protest regarding the refuse and pollution and formed the Anchors Away Citizen Group. Council approached the National Harbours Board (NHB) to enforce its own bylaws to no avail. Some local boat owners got caught in this fight. NHB lodged an appeal against a federal court judgement ordering it to evict houseboats and other illegally moored vessels in Deep Cove, and Anchors to Stay was formed. In August 1978 the DNV called for the removal of the vessels or threatened legal action. Most of the vessels quietly sailed into the sunset or sunk.

Condominiums: The first building permit for condominium development was issued for Deep Cove Crescent in 1970. By the 1980s development fever was heating up again and residents were calling for a Deep Cove plan. Councillor Ernie Crist says, "No area in the District has been studied more than Deep Cove."

The *Deep Cove Crier* reports strong opposition by Bill Blakely, David Breckner and Bill Prowse (to name a few local residents), who attended many council meetings attempting to keep development to a minimum. However, the following buildings were eventually completed:

Coveside, built in 1981 and located at the southwest corner of Gallant and Panorama; Panorama Place town homes, built in 1981; Cove Gardens, built in 1983 and

Illegally moored houseboats began appearing in the early 1970s. *Courtesy Marilyn Myers, 1319*

located at Naughton and Panorama; Deep Cove Condominium, located at 4389–91 Gallant Avenue; Mariners' Cove, built in 1984 and located at 2151 Banbury Road; Lions Manor seniors' complex, built in 1987 on the site of the original Deep Cove Community Hall, operated by the Mount Seymour Lions Club and offering units subsidized primarily on a rent-based-on-income principle with BC Housing; Deep Cove Estates condominium apartments and commercial units, built in 1991 and located at the northwest 400-block of Gallant Avenue.

The new houses today, especially those located on the original site of early cottages, are naturally larger and unfortunately for some that "Quaint Cove" atmosphere is disappearing.

Schools

Les Petites Amis French Kindergarten: From 1969 to 1989 Collette Mikhail, who immigrated to Canada from France, operated a French kindergarten in the basement of the old United Church building on Deep Cove Road.

My Little School: My Little School has been part of the Deep Cove community since 1991. Located in the old United Church building, it provides daycare programs for under-threes, a Montessori preschool and before and after school care for up to grade five. The school is operated by Karim Devraj.

Mamalina's Montessori Preschool: Yasmin Petigara opened this preschool in 1994 at 4317 Gallant Avenue. She brought

Deep Cove United Church ladies in the 1950s, prior to the building becoming My Little School. Left to right: Mrs. E.H. Bond, Ethel Yorke, Audrey Steele, Peggy Alway, Hazel Booth, Marge Wells, Ida White, Gladys Tobin, unidentified. *Courtesy Eileen Smith, 0964*

eighteen years of experience, preparation and training, and is a qualified Association Montessori Internationale (AMI) directress.

Merchants

Deep Cove has always been a tough location for merchants to operate a successful business. Over the last fifty years dozens of small storefront operations have opened and closed their doors. John Moore of the original Moore family, the first merchants in the Cove, had dreams of building a first-class hotel/restaurant/marina on the waterfront where the Deep Cove Yacht Club is located today, but local opposition to his scheme sent him away a very disappointed man.

As the population grew and became more mobile, supporting local business waned. Many who operated long-term businesses had connections elsewhere: Ron Yen's butcher shop and Milt and Margie Goodman's photo studios had a downtown customer base and Pavlik Travel also had clients from far afield.

Being at the "end of the road" doesn't help, especially in wet winter weather. But in 1974 chef Wolfgang Goudriaan and maître d'Augusto Pecorelli truly put Deep Cove on the map when they opened the Savoury Restaurant. Their promotional efforts over the years brought many new customers to the Cove for their legendary rack of lamb Djakarta.

In the 1990s Vlad Pabis purchased Honey Doughnuts from Helena Antkiewz and through his extensive advertising downtown he had people lining up for these tasty treats in no time. Mention Deep Cove and people from afar will still say, "Oh yes, that's where Honey Doughnuts is." It is currently owned and operated by Ashak and Ashifa Saferali.

Gradually, small shops appeared along Gallant Avenue. The village of Deep Cove thrived, as it began catering to more and more permanent residents.

A 1950s *Personal Recipes* cookbook published by the Women's Association of the Deep Cove United Church showed the following local advertisers: Red & White Store, Jack and Annie Huxham; Deep Cove Pharmacy, E.A. Worsley; Deep Cove Boat Rentals; Richards' (Ready to Wear

Mr. Gillis and Mr. Huxum, 1950s. Courtesy Clara Bliss, 2123

Footwear), run by the Richards family (later Jean's Variety and Deep Cove Variety); Eunice's Beauty Shop (Eunice Klassen) on Myrtle Avenue (now Naughton); and Pat's Coffee Bar (later Baldwin's and now the Deep Cove Cultural Centre).

Not advertised in the recipe book but well known in the Cove at that time were: Mollard's Market, Jimmy and Irma Mollard, son Ross and in-store butcher Mr. Elliott; Log Cabin Inn, a restaurant on the southwest corner of what is now Gallant and Banbury; and Dryhurst Electric, in the building that became The Establishment.

The Establishment, SW corner of Gallant Avenue and Panorama Drive. Courtesy Marilyn Myers, 1329

The following businesses were operating on Gallant Avenue in 1975: Panorama Market; Deep Cove Drugs; Deep Cove Pizza; Library on Gallant; Century Music Studios; The Owl Teahouse; Deep Cove Variety Store (Ron and Lucy Yen); butcher Jack Threlfall; General Grocery Store (Mr. Cho); Bowser Boutique Dog Grooming Salon; Macrame Studio; Pavlik Specialized Tours & Travel (opened in 1976); The Old Curiosity Shop (Mrs. Ramsay); The Savoury Restaurant (Wolfgang Goudriaan and Augusto Pecorelli); Andres Hair

The gang who occupied The Establishment. Left to right: Bob James, Andy Sloss, Darcy Rutherford, Pam Ciencella (now Rutherford), Gary Martin and Bob Duvernet. Courtesy Adrian Schweitzer, 4579-01

Above left: Cove View Court Motel (a.k.a. Deep Cove Motel) boat rentals. Courtesy Joe Thornley, 0649

Above right: Deep Cove Variety Store (formerly Jean's Variety and previously Richards' Ready to Wear Footwear), 1970s. Courtesy Ron Yen, 1770

Design (Barry and Donna Newcombe since the 1960s); Nutshell Restaurant; Goodman Photo Studios; Deep Cove Bike Shop.

Businesses operating in Deep Cove in 2011: Arms Reach Bistro, Alistair Knox & Erick Bullen; Mamalinas Montessori Preschool, Yasmin Petigara; First Mate Pet Foods, Mike Florian; Cove Realty, Anthea Yeo; Honeys Doughnuts, Ashak and Ashifa Saferali; La La's, Kristina Egyed; Osaka Sushi, Sy bae; Adriatic Travel and Cruise Centre, Mile Brkic; Deep Cove Pizza, Deborah and Peter Milcak; Deep Cove Pharmacy (Rexall), Fehmina Lalani, Arif Datoo and Lani Ha; Rita's Hair Design, Rita Le; Kuddle Muddle; Mystic Wardrobe, Anne-Marie Clark; Studio 6; Deep Cove Ice Cream; Turtle Restaurant; Mediterranean Restaurant, Houshang (Shawn) Memerzadeh; Deep Cove Bubble Tea, Kathy Park; Deep Cove Fish and Chips (Chang Lim).

Deep Cove Merchants' Association: In the 1980s Russell Davie, who operated the Gold and Silver Design shop, served as chairperson of the association. A meeting in April 1986 was attended by Susan MacDonald, Peter Taverner, Stan Hilckmann, Denis Fillion, Ron Yen, John Poon, Ingrid Baxter, Helena Antkiewz and Shirley Kubig. Among the items on the agenda was the Log Cabin heritage building, attracting a bank, advertising during Expo, Deep Cove Stage, Deep Cove Daze and old-fashioned lampposts.

It has been hard to keep the Merchants' Association active with such a frequent turnover of businesses over the years and lack of funds to complete some of the ambitious plans they have always dreamed of. In 2007 a meeting showed representatives from the following businesses: Kuddle Muddle, Room 6, Arms Reach and Deep Cove Kayak. Items on the agenda included farmers' market, lights in the trees, filming

The Savoury Restaurant. Photo by Adrian Schweitzer, 0889

in the Cove, signage, traffic, parking and hanging baskets.

Profiles

The Nutshell: The Nutshell, a local take-out restaurant, was a famous landmark by the dock in Deep Cove. People came by boat to experience the best hamburgers in town. Hilda and Al Bliss opened the Nutshell in the 1950s. Owners in the 1960s were Fred and Ann Hrychiw, and in the 1970s Bud Graves. He was followed by Stan Hilckmann, who introduced evening dining.

In 1988 Clara Bliss ran the restaurant for a year, prior to the building being sold and pulled down for new development. Cove Estate condos opened in 1989 and the Savoury Restaurant moved into the corner retail space.

In the late 1990s the restaurant was sold to Laurent Neveu and renamed the Eiffel Café. Alistair Knox and partner chef Erick Bullen purchased the business in 2004. Renamed Arms Reach Bistro, the restaurant continues the Nutshell tradition of excellence. Many patrons from Vancouver come to dine by the sea.

Cho Ning: Mr. Cho and his wife Maylene have owned Panorama Market since 1970 when he purchased Lupton's General Store (previously known as Mollards Market). He has always been a very community-minded man and he and his family

The Nutshell went from being an ice cream stand in the 1950s to a fine dining restaurant in the 1980s. Photo by George Turk, 4429

The Deep Cove Bike Shop later changed its name to Cove Bikes. Courtesy Terry Tobin, 1760

provided the Cove with merchandise not available at that time. In his retirement Mr. Cho enjoys his garden and his Chinese zucchini are famous. The store is presently leased to other operators.

Geoff Mortimer: Geoff came to Deep Cove around 1947 and in 1961 he owned and operated Deep Cove Drugs on Gallant Avenue. He became a well-loved member of the community and was known for his regular chess sessions at the back of the store. Indeed the drugstore was the local meeting place of the day. Geoff collected used books and started a mini library. He wrote newspaper articles and his poetry reflects his love of the Cove. He died in his Banbury home in a fire in 1995.[75]

Gallant Avenue was bustling even back in the mid-1980s. Photo by George Turk, 4428

"Sunday, February 11, 1973"
by Geoff Mortimer

Builders of houses, or weavers of rugs,
Healers of health, or dispensers of drugs,
Tillers of soil, or sailors of sea,
The folks of the Cove have serenity.
In a world of confusion, with so much sound,
It's healthful to have such havens around,
Where nature's baffles of rock and trees,
Absorb the noises which tear and tease.
So it isn't surprising folks grow old
Where the nights are pleasant and days aren't cold,
Where balm to the spirit lurks in the air,
And mental ease is everywhere.

Above: Hoisting a lamppost on Gallant, 1970s. Photo by Adrian Schweitzer, 4579-10

Left: Geoff and Florence Mortimer. Courtesy Doug Mortimer, 4593

Jan Stimpson: Jan started out as a fabric merchant. In 1980 she introduced a groundbreaking collection of washable silk designs under the Harmony label, which she retailed through her local store on Gallant Avenue. Her fashions were featured at Expo 86 and marketed from New York to Japan. Her label Chaos for Kids was launched in 1987 and she represented Canada with five other designers at the Osaka Expo in Japan. Her current collection Sympli is designed and manufactured in Vancouver and wholesaled across North America to over 900 retail stores.

Ron Yen: Ron owned and operated Suburban Farms on Gallant Avenue from 1972 to 1992. Ron, a qualified butcher by trade, butchered and packaged whole animals (popular freezer items at this time)

Deep Cove merchants, 2009. Ryan Crocker Photography, 4056

and had clients all over Vancouver (actor Bruno Gerussi and Judge Judy Morrison were regulars). Locally he was well known for his Maui ribs.

Wife Lucy Yen operated Jean's Variety Store and post office, which she took over from Dorothy Murrey across the street. Her selection of rubber boots was highly sought after.

Recreation

Everyone associates Deep Cove with recreation, whether sunning or swimming at the beach in summer or sailing, boating, kayaking and canoeing. Deep Cove is also a favourite haunt for hikers looking for the Baden Powell Trail and the trail to Quarry Rock is legendary.

There are no hotels or motels, only a few choice bed and breakfasts, and parking is a huge challenge for visitors and residents alike.

In the 1920s and 1930s the Deep Cove Regatta was a major summer event sponsored by the city of Vancouver. The year 1949 saw the birth of the North Arm Community Association. The goal of the association was "to promote and develop varied educational, athletic, dramatic, social and neighbourhood programs in order to develop community neighbourliness and good citizenship." Looking at the Cove today they certainly succeeded. Charter members included Margaret Berry, Hazel Booth, Margaret Davis, Ralph Fuller, John

Rawlins, Norman Black, George Taylor, Rex Eaton and Ethel Allardice.

Deep Cove North Shore Marina: Located at the end of Panorama Drive where Burrard Inlet and Indian Arm Inlet meet, the marina offers public boat moorage, fuel, a convenience store, docking facilities and boat rentals.

Originally owned and operated by Art George, it was known as Deep Cove Marina and then later as Seycove Marina. In 1993 the marina and surrounding land went through major development. Several high-end residential homes were built above the marina. Concerns from residents of Indian Arm Inlet were voiced at losing docking and moorage space.

Above: Art and Betty George at Deep Cove Marina (later renamed Seycove Marina), 1959. Courtesy Chevron Corporation, 4643

Below: Deep Cove North Shore Marina, 2010. 3628

Deep Cove Yacht Club (DCYC)

Piper leading Sail Past participants to the Deep Cove Yacht Club, with Mayor Marilyn Baker at front right, May 1984. Courtesy John Hutchinson, 2903

Deep Cove Clearwater Committee: The 1979 Deep Cove Clearwater Committee report cited several problems with the proposal to move the Deep Cove Yacht Club including: a net loss of approximately 245 m (800 ft) of shoreline on the Deep Cove waterfront; increased pressure on limited parking spaces; increased traffic in residential areas with potential danger for children as the new Cove Cliff Elementary School was to be built at the intersection of Banbury and Raeburn streets; encroachment on wilderness park areas and negative impact on small bird and animal habitat; destruction of the major canoeing area in Deep Cove by converting public space to private space; reduction of

CHRONOLOGY—DEEP COVE YACHT CLUB

1936 Deep Cove Yacht Club (DCYC) is officially registered on July 31 as the Deep Cove Yacht and Sports Club

1938 Members clear land in Panorama Park, and erect clubhouse building

Second World War clubhouse used for Ladies' Air Raid Patrol & Red Cross Auxiliary

1943 The Deep Cove Sports Association becomes the Deep Cove Yacht and Sports Club. Clubhouse building is vacated and turned over to North Vancouver Municipality for use as an elementary school during the war

1979 Proposals for the move of the DCYC to the current Deep Cove Park water frontage

Deep Cove Clearwater Committee files report against the DCYC move, "Report on Future Marine Development in Deep Cove," with the DNV

DCYC ultimately does not move; old Yacht Club pier is demolished and replaced by new piles and a new decking

1980 Club installs three new water ballasted concrete floats

1982 Pier extended, and new aluminum ramp installed

1984 New clubhouse is built[76, 77]

Boat races in Deep Cove, ca. 1950s. Courtesy Arthur and Vivienne Coverdale, 1407

swimming area; loss of aesthetic quality of Deep Cove through cluttering the harbour with marinas and mooring.

The report also cited several public benefits from the relocation of the DCYC: land in Panorama Park would be freed; potential for the public to make use of the DCYC clubhouse.

The report suggested several alternatives to moving the DCYC to Deep Cove Park, most notably moving the club to Cates Park.[78]

Speed Boat Races: Locals will remember the roar of powerful motors echoing around the Cove as the local Kinsmen and Vancouver Power Boat Association organized the Gold Cup motor boat races in 1954. Over 10,000 spectators contributed to the Kinsmen coffers and to the local economy.

Deep Cove Canoe & Kayak Centre: Ingrid Baxter and Merv Ovesen expanded the operation to include kayaks. Today it is one of the leading paddling locations in Vancouver.

Under the management of Bob Putnam since 1996, the company has kept up to date by introducing new water sports such as stand-up paddle boarding and surf ski paddling. The rowing club participates in all major rowing events. Dragon boat races are an annual event in the Cove.

Old Deep Cove Yacht Club before demolition, December 1984. Courtesy Marilyn Myers, 1327

CHRONOLOGY—DEEP COVE CANOE & KAYAK

1940s Picturesque waterfront log cabins (believed to have been built by local entrepreneur Alfred "Shorty" Riebolt) are located on the current site of the Deep Cove Park and Canoe & Kayak boathouse

1948 Doc Miller from San Francisco operates an exclusive boys' summer camp. Reportedly a son of Bing Crosby attended

1950s Joe and Reta Thornley convert the cabins to the Deep Cove Motel and operate for twenty years. They also build a wharf, Panorama Park Marina, located south of the current government wharf

1970s The DNV reclaims the land now called Deep Cove Park. Cabins (except one) and wharf are demolished

1986 Last cabin finally demolished. Ingrid Baxter, who had lived there and operated Deep Cove Canoe Rentals, said: "It's more of a historic loss to the community." Merchants and others were unsuccessful at lobbying the District to retain this building

1989 The District constructs a new boathouse, the present home of Deep Cove Canoe & Kayak and the Deep Cove Rowing Club

2005 Deep Cove Outdoors retail opens

Cove Water Sports: Founded in 2003 by owner Joel Perkins, the company claims to be BC's largest wakeboard school and offers wakeboarding, wakeskating and wakesurfing.

Deep Cove Canoe & Kayak building. 4580

Kayak race in the Cove, ca. 1987. 0958

Hiking: The Baden Powell Trail spans the North Shore from Deep Cove to Horseshoe Bay commencing (or finishing) at a point at the end of Panorama Park. The trail was blazed by the Boy Scouts as a Centennial project in 1967. Records show the Golden Age Hiking club assisted in maintaining the trail over the years and built a set of new stairs. Hundreds of hikers are seen any time of the year on the section from Deep Cove to the Rock (Quarry Rock).

Government Wharf: Government Wharf was originally built by the Department of Transport Marine Services and rebuilt by the same in the early 1970s. Initially the wharf was an extension of a provincially owned dedicated public road allowance. The District owns the wharves at Sunshine Falls, Woodlands, Strathcona and Cates Park.

Community Facilities and Events

Deep Cove Community Hall: The community hall was the heart of the Cove for many years. A lack of churches, schools, firehall and other public facilities made this hall the essential meeting place for the area and it served the community well.

CHRONOLOGY—DEEP COVE COMMUNITY HALL

1935 A shed for the hose and reel served as location for a firehall

1941 Community hall and garage for a fire truck is built with volunteer labour by the Deep Cove/Dollarton Rate Payers' Association

1941–55 All church denominations use the hall, which also serves as a library and kindergarten

A caretaker is hired and the hall rented for parties and dances

1960–70s Used for a variety of community purposes including YWCA programs, martial arts and exercise classes

mid-1970s The Community Association turns the running of the hall over to the District

1976–87 The Deep Cove Stage Association leases the hall, builds a theatre with raised seating and produces four plays a year including their famous Christmas pantomimes

1987 Hall is demolished to make way for Lions Manor seniors' complex

Above: Deep Cove Community Hall, 1987. 4028

Deep Cove/Dollarton Community Association: Although the association is no longer active, in the past a group of concerned citizens always quickly formed when alerted that there were pending changes in the community that would affect residents. In the 1970s Ray Eagle acted as watchdog in the neighbourhood; through the 1980s Bill Blakely frequented District Hall; today Trevor Carolan, Margie Goodman, Anthea Yeo and many others keep a close watch on the Cove.

Deep Cove Kinsmen: In the early days of Deep Cove the Kinsmen provided the social calendar for residents. See *Echoes Across the Inlet* for details on their influence and community work.

Come Home to the Cove Day: In 1976 the Deep Cove/Dollarton Community Association, headed up by Ray Eagle and Janet Pavlik, organized a fifty-year reunion day celebrating summer fun in the Cove.

Come Home to the Cove Day took place on August 7, 1976. Over 600 invitations were sent out by Eileen Elliott to ex-"Covites" in Canada, the US and Europe.

The day was opened by Chief John George and recaptured the spirit of past regattas with boating, swimming and canoe races. Water events were organized by Bob Wells of the DCYC, Mrs. Barlow and Mrs. Foreman of the Mount Seymour Swim Club and Art George of the Deep Cove Marina.

The day included musical entertainment, an archival exhibition organized by the Deep Cove Heritage Association, a nostalgic stage show, *The Five Wishes*, and a video of the 1936 Deep Cove Regatta courtesy of Linda Henrickson. The evening concluded with a raffle for two tickets to London. Deep Cove pioneer John Moore pulled the winning tickets for an excited crowd.

Deep Cove Daze: Community days have been a feature in Deep Cove since the early regattas in the Cove in the 1920s. The Kinsmen organized May Day celebrations and community days and the Mount Seymour Lions Club started an annual community day in the 1960s called King Neptune's Karnival. By the 1990s the event was renamed Deep Cove Daze and was run by the Merchants' Association. In 1997 Lisa Muri and others in the community organized the event. In 1998 Musart Cultural Society took over organizing. The event is held at the end of August with the main emphasis on established and emerging performing bands under the artistic direction of Tyler Pearson. Dave Crowe and Craig Johnston serve on the board of directors.

Deep Cove Daze, 1995. Courtesy Gillian Murray, 0826

Carol Ship Night: The carol ships Parade of Lights Society has been around for over fifty years. This spectacular parade of decorated boats is a Christmas tradition in Vancouver and includes West and North Vancouver. It is a magical sight as the boats come into Deep Cove to be greeted with a huge bonfire and carol singers on the beach.

In 1962 Milt Goodman and Jordon Welsh organized a Cove Carol Ship Night with Milt's boat, the *Goodship*. Art George distributed flares to houses on Panorama Drive that lit the way for the flotilla of local boats.

Concerts in the Cove: Organized by the District these concerts in the park are very popular family-oriented events. Locals enjoy the variety of music offered on Friday nights in the Cove during July and August.

First Light Over the Cove: The new millennium was welcomed with a special breakfast on January 1, 2000, at the Deep Cove Yacht Club, organized by the Deep Cove Heritage Society and followed by the

Opposite bottom: The firehall was built in 1953 (Gospel Hall Church parishioners in photo). Courtesy Wayne Smith, 1627

CHRONOLOGY—PENGUIN PLUNGE

1983 On New Year's Day Merv Ovesen and friends plunge into the waters in front of the Deep Cove Canoe & Kayak centre as an alternative to the Polar Bear Swim in Vancouver. Merv says it's much safer plunging in and out than swimming. Four plungers and a dog went in and the Penguin Plunge was launched

1984 Eighteen plungers and two dogs

1986 The location changes to Panorama Park Beach. North Vancouver Recreation Commission assists with the event, which sees forty-two plungers and their dogs go in, many in costumes, with hundreds of spectators

1991 The event mushrooms into a major event with the involvement of the Rec Commission, Deep Cove Yacht Club and Mount Seymour Lions. Family entertainment, a bonfire and refreshments are introduced

2000 A record number of locals and visitors plunge into freezing waters to bring in the new millennium

2011 After twenty-eight years the Penguin Plunge has become a New Year's Day Deep Cove treasured tradition. Over 450 plungers and 2,000 spectators were recorded in 2011. There was no dog count

unveiling of a plaque in Panorama Park to commemorate this special day.

Olympic Games Celebration: The arrival of the Olympic torch in Deep Cove set the scene for the largest turnout of residents the Cove had ever seen.

Deep Cove Cultural Centre: The Cultural Centre is the best thing that has happened to Deep Cove in the last fifty years. A fountain designed by Greg Kawczynski

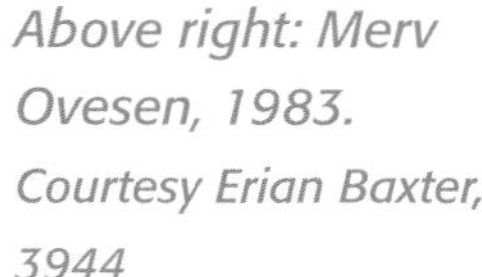

Above right: Merv Ovesen, 1983. Courtesy Erian Baxter, 3944

Right: Penguin Plunge, 2011. 4602

First Light Over the Cove plaque unveiling and crowd, January 1, 2000. DCHS, 2203

sits in the village square adjacent to the building, which has become the focus of community life in the village. Living in an area full of recreational opportunities, there was a real need to provide space for the many artists, musicians and thespians who choose to live here.

Mayor Marilyn Baker said in 1988: "There is no question but that a specially planned facility capable of housing quality shows and programs in the heart of Deep Cove will provide a major economic and social focus to the small commercial core and surrounding natural park and recreation amenities."[79]

The Deep Cove/Dollarton Community Programs minutes for that year indicate strong support for a new cultural centre. The DNV came up with the land and the Mount Seymour Lions Club donated $60,000 in exchange for the original community hall site, where Lions Manor seniors' complex was built. As Deep Cove Stage had lost its home, the seed of an idea for a Deep Cove cultural centre that could house it and four other "homeless" groups came from Ann Booth. First Impressions Theatre, Seymour Art Gallery, Deep Cove

Bottom: Olympic Torch at the foot of Gallant Street. Photo by Christina Kasperczyk, 4062

Above: Deep Cove Stage's 1995 Theatre BC Festival Winner, Look Back in Anger. *Clockwise from left: Catherine Watkins, Tierney Fyfe, Mark Gash, Mike Jarvis, Maggie Kolodziej, Ann Booth, Jenny Ashton, Damian Inwood, Roy Kaighin, and Ron Bashera; taken at Mainstage in Kamloops. Courtesy Deep Cove Stage Society, 4767*

and Area Heritage Society and the Deep Cove Chamber Soloists got together along with Deep Cove Stage, and the Deep Cove Cultural Society was formed.

It took four years of hard work and meetings to make the centre a reality. Those involved were Ann Booth, Damian Inwood, Michael and Eileen Smith, Sherrill Hardy, Sylvia and John Forrest, and Hazel Baxter from the District, among many others.

The 130-seat studio theatre component of the building was to be the shared home of the Deep Cove Stage Society and First Impressions Theatre. Because of the major grant provided by Shaw Communications it was named Deep Cove Shaw Theatre.[80]

Deep Cove Stage Society (DCSS): The DCSS has offered community theatre to the area since 1976. Early performances were at Burrard View School followed by memorable shows at the old Community Hall. Founding members were locals Trevor and Jill Adams, who brought their theatre experience from the UK. Pat Chetwynd, Pat Garland and Ann Booth are still actively involved. The group produces four shows a year; the annual Christmas pantomime always sells out and has become another treasured tradition in the Cove.

Right: First Impressions Theatre 2009 production of Office Hours. *Ryan Crocker Photography, 4693*

Left: Michael Smith (shown here), and Mike Jarvis (DCSS), pictured on opposite page, have worked at the centre since the start. Ryan Crocker Photography, 4772

First Impressions Theatre Society: Established in 1983 by talented thespian Neil Boucher along with Warde Ashlie (an actor from the Cove), Eric Rosen (a teacher at Burrard View School) and Cove residents Michael and Eileen Smith, the goal of First Impressions Theatre (FIT) was to provide a forum for performers of diverse backgrounds to explore and develop their creative potential in theatre, music and dance through public performance. They certainly have achieved those goals over the years.

Prior to having a permanent home, FIT performed at Burrard View School, the Deep Cove Stage community hall and Presentation House, and produced the Christmas show for ten years at James Cowan Theatre in Burnaby. As residents at the Deep Cove Shaw Theatre, the group produces up to four plays a year and one or two fundraising concerts, the proceeds of which go into upgrading theatre equipment. Concerts have featured Long John Baldry, Jim Byrnes, Roy Forbes, Babe Gurr, Bill Henderson, Shari Ulrich, Barney Bentall, Keith Bennett, Jocelyn Pettit and Charles van Sandwyck, among others. Like Deep Cove Stage, FIT supports itself from ticket sales and does not receive grants. FIT has hosted fundraisers for Seymour Art Gallery and Deep Cove Heritage and produced shows with Theatricks. For the last several years Darlene Manchester, Ryan Crocker, Rita Arhipov, Kelly Avery and Michael and Eileen Smith have worked on every production.

Founders Eileen and Michael Smith have lovingly devoted their lives to keeping the centre running smoothly.

Both FIT and the Deep Cove Stage Society have been involved with Theatre BC and won many awards.

Seymour Art Gallery: Officially established in 1985 under the Deep Cove/Dollarton Community Programs Society, the Seymour Art Gallery began its life with exhibitions in the corridors of the community wing at Seycove School.

The gallery provides space for regional artists and artist groups from amateur to professional and a gift shop space for selling local crafts. Educational programs are offered both in the schools and in-house. An elected board runs the gallery, with many hundreds of volunteers contributing to its success.

Instrumental to the success of the gallery are Joan and Ken Fowler. Joan was a

Below: Seymour Art Gallery's annual DisCOVEry exhibition, 2012. Courtesy Sarah Cavanaugh, 4770

CHRONOLOGY—SEYMOUR ART GALLERY

1984 Linda Moore, Community School coordinator, obtains a $37,000 Canada Employment Grant to establish the gallery

1985 Sherill Hardy is appointed gallery's first coordinator/curator and forms the Arts Committee. Roman Skotnicki designs the logo and area to be used

1986 Official ribbon cutting by MLA Jack Davis and Mayor Marilyn Baker

Heritage photo collection is donated by Janet Pavlik. Yvonne Prudek is made archival curator and the first exhibition, "Down Memory Lane," features heritage photos

1986 Local artists displaying their work: Ruth Coxon Lewis, Janus Janssens, Dennis Hutchins, Paul Buten, Susan McDonald, Dale Matthews, Cathy Fletcher, Lindsay Ross, Mary Bartlett, Eileen Dearden, Miriam McCulloough, Richard de la Mare, Hermione Green, Russel Davies, Ian S. Smart and Elizabeth George

1986–92 Twelve annual exhibitions feature many different mediums

1992 Seymour Art Gallery moves into its new home in the Deep Cove Cultural Centre

1993–2003 Carole Badgley is appointed administrator/curator and generates huge publicity for the gallery through her connections in the art world. Fundraising projects, Native Art, glass, printmaking and pastel exhibitions are some of her innovative ideas, along with the introduction of the Discovery Shows

2003–2010 Jacquie Morgan becomes curator. Her focus is emerging artists and textile arts

2010–present Curator is Sarah Cavanaugh

core volunteer for the gallery and head of the board for many years. Ken served as president. Their support of Arts in the Cove (introduced by Sandra Dent) continues to be appreciated by all groups in the cultural centre.

In keeping with the tradition of Deep Cove as cultural hub in the Seymour area two new galleries have recently opened in the village: Artemis, owned and operated by Shannon Browne; and Cove Creek Gallery, owned by Sharon Perkins. Bel Art Gallery at 2171 Deep Cove Road is owned by Beatrice and Stefan Schreiber.

Deep Cove Heritage Society: Originally known as the Deep Cove and Area Heritage Association, the society operated from a filing cabinet in the corridor of the community wing in Seycove School until 1985. For the full story please refer to the Deep Cove Heritage Society story in this book.

Deep Cove Chamber Soloists Society: The Chamber Soloists Society is a group of experienced professional musicians founded in 1983. Pro Nova Ensemble is its performing arm. The society's goals are to present original chamber music to audiences on the North Shore, to commission new works by regional and national composers and to promote Canadian classical music. Today they perform in venues such as the Mount Seymour United Church.

Musicians

Joelle Rabu: Born in Winnipeg and raised in Courtenay, BC, chanteuse Joelle Rabu grew up in the family restaurant trade. After travelling widely, she began performing her acclaimed bilingual role as Edith Piaf in concert at Vancouver's City Stage in 1983. Her show *Piaf, Her Songs Her Loves* electrified the city. Rabu lived on Panorama Drive in Deep Cove during the late 1980s. She continues to tour, often accompanied by her pianist and son, Nico Rhodes.

Rene Worst: Born in New Guinea, bassist Rene Worst moved to Canada with his family in 1960. A founding member of the jazz fusion group Skywalk that enjoyed a halcyon period in the 1980s, he appeared on six albums with them. Worst has also performed with David Bowie, Chet Baker, Rita MacNeil, Phoebe Snow and many others. During the late 1980s and 1990s he lived on Little Panorama Drive in Deep Cove, noting to friends that his house address—1967—was the same year that the Beatles' *Sgt. Pepper's Lonely Hearts Club Band* album was released. Worst continues to perform and record with his wife, vocalist/pianist Jennifer Scott, one of Canada's premier jazz artists.

Long John Baldry: While never an actual Seymour resident, Long John Baldry was no stranger here and generously offered his time and talent at fundraising concerts and telethons in support of the Deep Cove Cultural Centre. His still-talked-about "rave up" show with sideman guitarist Tony Robertson at the Raven Pub in the early 1990s, when the doors were locked early and Long John rocked away 'til the cows came home, showed why Rod Stewart's old boss was still one of the biggest stars in the constellation of English blues. An honorary local. Of note: Elton John took the name "John" from Long John Baldry.

Tony Robertson with legendary bluesman Long John Baldry in the Cultural Centre, July 1999. 0959

Jim Byrnes and Roy Forbes: Both men are highly respected, popular musicians who have been supporting the Deep Cove Cultural Centre and groups from the start and continue to do so by participating in fundraising concerts.

Keith Bennett: Deep Cove is home to the multi-talented musical skills of Keith Bennett. He is a veteran singer and instrumentalist and was known for eight years as the Harmonica Man at Vancouver Canucks hockey games. His range of music is amazing: he has performed classical with the Vancouver Symphony Orchestra and blues, country and jazz at top Canadian venues. Keith is featured on over 200 CDs and soundtracks for film and television.

Right: Trevor Carolan with Jean Craig. Courtesy Trevor Carolan, 1029

Keith Bennett, a regular supporter of Deep Cove Heritage Society. Courtesy Keith Bennett, 4600

Writers

Trevor Carolan: Author and poet Trevor Carolan first visited Dollarton in 1960 after his father performed in a local theatre production with Dan George. On moving to Deep Cove in 1989 he and his wife rallied other Seymour media veterans to help end the pollution problems that plagued the bay. Carolan's many books and interviews with prominent artists and spiritual leaders are published internationally, and his acclaimed *Return to Stillness: Twenty Years With a Tai Chi Master* contains vivid local imagery. After his role with GUARD in protecting East Seymour's Cove and Mountain forests, Carolan served on the DNV council from 1996 to 1999 and became a popular political columnist for the *North Shore News.*

Peter Newman: Former editor of the *Toronto Star* and *Maclean's* magazine, Newman has been the ongoing chronicler of the lives of Canada's business and political elites for decades. He lived on Panorama Drive in Deep Cove during the early 1990s, and visitors there recall his love for playing loud Stan Kenton jazz and the sight of his lead-lined, snoop-proof filing cabinets. An avid sailor, his yacht was one of the most recognizable vessels in local waters.

Neil Freeman: A professional actor, director and author of books on Shakespeare, including the 1,200-page acclaimed *Applause First Folio of Shakespeare in Modern Type: Comedies, Histories and Tragedies*, Neil lived for many years on Caledonia overlooking the water. He is the Associate Professor Emeritus in the Department of Theatre Film and Creative Writing at UBC.

Bill Gaston: Born in Flin Flon, Manitoba, novelist Bill Gaston was partly raised in the Seymour area, where his mother, Mary, was a popular Deep Cove realtor. *Deep Cove Stories,* his first volume of fiction published in 1989, draws on the area for inspiration. In his sparkling story "The Forest Path to Malcolm's," the narrator purports to be the illegitimate son of Malcolm Lowry. Gaston's many books have been nominated for national awards. He teaches at the University of Victoria.

Crawford Killian: After immigrating to Canada from California in the 1960s, author Crawford Killian taught for forty years at Capilano College, now Capilano University, prior to his retirement in 2008. He has published many books, mainly in the realm of speculative fiction, as well as scores of articles on education, science, the environment, politics and writing for new media. Currently he writes for the online newspaper, *The Tyee*, in Vancouver and is an active blogger.

Shelley Harrison Rae: A long-time resident of Deep Cove with her family, Shelley now lives on the Sunshine Coast. She was the coordinator and a volunteer for the Deep Cove Heritage Society in the early 2000s. Shelley has made a life writing and guiding other writers to find their voice and develop their craft with workshops here and in Rancho La Puerta Spa in Tecate, Mexico. A writer, editor and manuscript coach, she has self-published a book of poetry called *Life Leaves Stains* and continues to write for the *Deep Cove Crier.*

Shelley Harrison Rae. *Photo by Mike Wakefield,* North Shore News, *2959*

Frank Roosen: A book titled *A True Life Story*, by Frank Roosen, recalls his life and chronicles his many years in Deep Cove. In the 1960s he had a bakery business and delivered bread across the Seymour area. A local handyman, he worked overtime to support his family. As bread increased in price people started to bake their own and Frank moved on to purchase an oil business from Oscar and Omar Hanson and named it Roosen Fuel. Certainly a character, his Jake the Peg three-legged skit was bought by Australian comedian Rolf Harris who used it for his cabaret openings.

Artists

Charles van Sandwyk: Charles van Sandwyk was raised in Deep Cove from

Right: "Ratty Ventures Into Wild Wood" by Charles van Sandwyk, from The Wind in the Willows. *Courtesy Charles van Sandwyk, 4583*

Below: Charles van Sandwyk with his first street banners, 2011. 4582

the age of twelve and lives in one of the few remaining uniquely charming original Cove cottages. His highly detailed precision paintings and etchings (printed on his antique press) have details usually reserved for scientific illustration, if it were not for their subject matter. Gossamer fairies, elves, owls, woodland creatures and gentle majestic animals with wit and charm invite you into their world. Charles also produces books, both by hand (for small editions) or through publishers (for larger editions). He shares some of the work of framing, printing of etchings and bookbinding with Waisiki Doughty, co-author of their book *Canadian Content.* Charles illustrated the *Blue Fairy Book, The Wind in the Willows* and *Alice in Wonderland* for the British Folio Society. His work is collected across North America and Europe and is archived in the National Library of Canada.

Graham Eagle: Brought up in Deep Cove, Graham has always been a unique individual. His marvellous quick wit immediately puts you at ease. From a career in architecture he became a full-time artist in 1994. His whimsical sculptures in wood, watercolour paintings and photography reflect his great ability to recycle all kinds of mediums and his work can be found in private and corporate collections worldwide.

Rudy Lechleter: Born in Germany, Rudy began his art training at age seventeen, which ranged from graphic art to mural painting. In 1970 he immigrated to Canada and was introduced to the basics of working on metal surfaces such as brass, copper and aluminum. By 1973 he had started his own studio. His work is currently exhibited and sold in the US, Germany and Canada. From his beautiful home on Panorama Drive in Deep Cove he and Marijo Baehr operate Seaside Lookout bed and breakfast. His works are exhibited at the Bel Art Gallery.

Graham Eagle's custom wood sculpture On the Rocks with Arthur Erickson. *Courtesy Graham Eagle, 2154*

Larry Lillo: One of the Vancouver theatre world's most beloved characters, Larry Lillo was co-founder of Tamahnous Theatre in 1971. An impassioned director and actor he became artistic director of the Vancouver Playhouse in 1988 and audience memberships soared. Larry lived at the north end of Panorama Drive in Deep Cove. He passed on too soon in 1993 and his partner, John Moffat, followed in 1995.

People

The Cove is crawling with interesting people. The community has attracted many characters over the years and has become a haven for artists, writers, intellectuals, hippies, musicians and even a few draft dodgers during the 1970s. Today those professionals who can afford a multi-million-dollar home on the waterfront commute to downtown Vancouver and come home to the serenity of the Cove.

Bill Blakely: Long-time president and driving force of the Deep Cove Community Association, Bill was a community planner and involved with the siting of Simon Fraser University atop Burnaby Mountain. He pioneered the use of the alternating double-lane on Lions Gate Bridge. An environmental and heritage warrior he fought many a battle on behalf of the Cove.[81]

Fredrick Robert McKee: Fondly known as the Mayor of Deep Cove, Fred came to Canada from Ireland in 1956 and could be always seen in Deep Cove wearing "his green." He worked for the DNV in the 1960s followed by a stint with Roosen

Above: Bill and Betty Blakely. Courtesy Betty Blakely, 4705

Top right: Fredrick Robert McKee. Courtesy Peggy McKee, 3207

Right: Fred Senft, left, and Dan Miskinac. 4607

Opposite: Jan Overby. 4606

Fuels. In more recent years he worked for Deep Cove Pizza.

Cove Custodians: Deep Cove presently has three gentlemen who take great pride in keeping the Cove clean and tidy. Jan Overby, known as the current Mayor of the Cove, can be seen in the village early in the morning with his broom. Fred Senft makes sure bottles and cans are collected around the Cove and park areas. Park keeper Dan Miskinac does a valiant job cleaning up after the thousands of visitors who frequent the Cove each year.

Clara Bliss: Clara grew up in Deep Cove and still lives here today. She has involved herself with many local activities and was especially influential in decision-making with parent groups at Burrard View School, where her four children attended. Heading up the committee to bring about the new Seycove Secondary School, her enthusiasm and infectious laugh helped the process along. Clara was also the popular bartender at The Raven Pub for many years.

Dr. Lyle Thurston: A long-time Deep Cove resident, Dr. Lyle Thurston was widely respected as a physician within the BC arts and environmental communities for his unconventional approaches to good health. His overgrown cottage near the entrance to the Baden Powell Trail on Panorama Drive featured quirky metal art around his front yard from the set of the original *Star Wars* film. In *Warriors of the Rainbow*, Greenpeace founder Bob Hunter writes of Thurston's wacky, heroic spirit as ship doctor, while aboard the first Greenpeace anti-nuclear testing expedition to Alaska in 1971. Thurston lived large. He died in Victoria in 2008.

Hazel Best: A resident of the Cove since 1942, Hazel's razor-sharp memory has provided so many stories and changes over the years. An active member of the Heritage Society her volunteer work has been recognized by Guides, Brownies, seniors, parent-teacher associations and the United Church, to name a few. She has three kids, eleven grandchildren and twenty-three great-grandchildren, many of whom live in the Seymour area. Hazel remembers the area being cleared—there was little or no hardpan and building lots were very wet and soggy. She recalls that with no major local stores, catalogue buying was popular.

Damian Inwood: Journalist Damian Inwood came to Canada from the UK in 1973. He and his family eventually made Deep Cove home and he has worked for the Vancouver *Province* newspaper for a number of years. Always active in the

Damian Inwood and Tom Boogers with the Deep Cove Heritage Millennium plaque, 2000. 4200

community, Damian headed up the Deep Cove and Area Heritage Association for ten years, during which time the group published *Echoes Across the Inlet*, edited by Damian. He is a long-standing member of the Deep Cove Stage Society and an accomplished actor and director. Being part of the Deep Cove pantomime scene, he is also well known for his "Dame" performances and singing with the North Shore Chorus.

Bill Cameron: The Neil Squire Society was founded by Deep Cove local Bill Cameron in June 1984 and had offices on Gallant Avenue. For more than twenty-five years the society has empowered over 20,000 Canadians with physical disabilities through the use of computer-based assistive technologies, research and development and various employment programs.[82]

It would take another book to share all the stories and backgrounds of the interesting people who have made the Cove home, and that have been collected over four years of interviews and reading newspaper stories and books. Please visit the Deep Cove Heritage Society collection, which includes the Thornley, Elliott, Dobson, Jenkins, George, Goodman, Beniston, Bartlett, Bullen, McKay, Brechner, Cameron, Phillips, Alway, Foreman, Inkstir, Helliwell, Harper, Scott and Wells families. You just might find out more of your own family history there.

Environment

Known for its heavy rainfalls—205 to 230 cm (80 to 90 inches) annually at sea level—Deep Cove boasts greenery throughout the year. The Who's Got the Umbrella water fountain in the village square is aptly named.

Framed by the tall fir trees on Mount Seymour we are reminded how close we are to our four-legged neighbours who visit us regularly. Bear sightings are common and regular Bear Watch programs attempt to educate us on how to live alongside one another.

It has been said that there are more dogs than people in the Cove. This seems to be the case as you observe the nightly parade of dogs and owners circling Panorama Park come rain or shine.

Water Pollution: Janet Pavlik claims to have swum each summer in the Cove for over forty years. However, there have been years when there was much controversy on the safety of the water in the Cove.

In 1985 Panorama Park Beach was closed due to a high coliform count reaching 1,240 (acceptable limit 200). The following year senior health inspector Bill Kimmett cited Fraser River agricultural sewage leaking into Deep Cove via tidal flow as the problem.

Local resident Noel van Sandwyk wrote in the *North Shore News* of toilet paper sightings and blamed boaters. By 1988 the beach was closed for forty-seven days; this time storm sewers and creeks were blamed. Even the local dog population was blamed for the pollution.

In 1989 the local community was determined to get answers to the water problems. The Community Association met with the DNV Technical Steering Committee comprised of members from Environment Canada, Fisheries and Oceans, the Greater Vancouver Regional District, UBC Institute for Aquaculture Research and the Port Authority. Among the topics discussed were water sampling and the effect of local fish farms on the coliform count.

In 1990 the Community Association and the DNV announced that urban runoff was the cause of the high coliform count. In 1997 a Pollution Prevention Program was implemented in an attempt to abate the coliform count in urban runoff streams.

Dog walkers: Eliska Khashan with Kuko; Russ Curtis with Yogi and Tyke; John Fowler with Fritz and Chase. 4622

In 1989 Barrie C. Brundage wrote an open letter to the DNV via the *North Shore News* entitled "Pollution is a dog-gone problem":

> Congratulations regarding the coliform count. You finally caught the culprit—the local dog! Not the cats, deer, geese, bear, humans or the budgies. It is essential that you not blame the ducks, seagulls and geese as you are unable to create bylaws to contain these creatures. Several questions come to mind, do weekend yachts coincide with the coliform count? Possibly the yachts have dogs on board. Why is toilet paper floating in the Cove? Believe me, dogs are not that well trained . . . If I promise to shoot my dog will you promise to repair the sewer system, check the septic tanks, stop yachts, kill all the birds, animals and fish, remove two-thirds of the houses on Panorama and increase the tidal action to "flush" the Cove?

Deep Cove for Separation

On April 1, 1977, local resident Frances Gray wrote:

> It seems that the recent victory of the Parti Québecois has awakened hitherto unsuspected passions in many of the residents of Deep Cove. A committee for an independent Deep Cove is being formed.
>
> Preliminary meetings have been held to set up areas of study regarding the financing. The Federal Government has been approached regarding a feasibility study and the Provincial Government has been asked to fund these studies.
>
> There seems no doubt that Deep Cove would be financially independent. In fact it could run with a considerable profit from its floating casino offshore. Deep Cove would apply to Great Britain, the USA, Canada, Cuba and Uganda for aid as an underdeveloped nation. OPEC countries would be approached for money to look for oil. Big business would, of course, have P.O. Boxes to establish addresses in Deep Cove as a tax haven. Tourism would boom with people flocking to see the smallest nation in North America. As cash flowed in there would be no taxes for the residents of the principality of Deep Cove.[83]

Chapter 19

Multi-community

The Seymour area has come a long way in the last fifty years, from small, scattered communities along the shores of Burrard Inlet to developed neighbourhoods stretching from industrial Maplewood to the popular scenic village of Deep Cove. This chapter is intended to give you an idea of services and facilities available in Seymour and how things have evolved to the life we have today.

Newsletters and Newspapers

Reading through newsletters of the 1940s, '50s and '60s is great fun and you truly get a good feel for the times. Local business advertisements show how the community relied on their services. To take a look and "read all about it," call into the Deep Cove Heritage office to see these interesting publications: *North Arm News*; North Shore communities newsletter; *Deep Cove News*, 1947 Bulletins; the *Citizen* column "Around Deep Cove"; *Times* of North and West Vancouver; *North Shore News*; the *Outlook*; the *Seymour Eagle* (Seymour Community Association); *Deep Cove Crier*, the current voice of Seymour. Our heritage office has the largest and an almost complete collection of this paper.

Bruce Coney founded the *Deep Cove Crier* in 1987 with the help of daughter Janine. Born in Durban, South Africa, Bruce and his family immigrated to Canada in 1982 and lived in Deep Cove from 1982 to 2001. He worked in the newspaper industry in Vancouver as the advertising director of the *West Ender*. In 1990 he launched the *West End Times*, a community newspaper in the West End and downtown Vancouver. Bruce sold both newspapers to the North Shore News Group in 1999, but he and Janine still publish the *Deep Cove Crier*.

Bruce now resides on Salt Spring Island, where he runs a glass and pottery studio.

Janine and Bruce Coney of the Deep Cove Crier, *2011. 4623*

Opposite top: Soccer Coach Bob Moss teaches a class in Myrtle Park. Photo Cindy Goodman, North Shore News, *4210*

Opposite middle: North Shore Girls Soccer, 2012. Courtesy Pro-Line Sports Photography, 4666

Opposite bottom: Mount Seymour Little League, 1990. Courtesy Janet Pavlik, 1505

Television and Film

This area is very much part of "Hollywood North." Where else can film crews find wilderness with backdrop scenery such as ours only thirty minutes from downtown Vancouver? The Seymour area has become home for many television series including *Danger Bay*, *The X-Files* and *Men in Trees*.

Donnelly Rhodes: Raised in Winnipeg, actor Donnelly Rhodes became one of the West Coast's most familiar television personalities through his ongoing role as Dr. Grant Roberts, a marine biologist, on the popular Canadian family series *Danger Bay*. Filmed at the Indian Arm waterfront community of Woodlands, the long-running program's success (1985–90) helped eclipse his previous work in the daytime soap opera *The Young and the Restless* during the 1970s. His recent work includes the film *Battlestar Galactica* and he's still seen around the Sunshine Coast.

Andy Smith: Deep Cove resident Andy Smith has made a name for himself in the movie business with his ingenious car designs. His special effects include the Batmobile in the movie *Batman Begins.* He built historic racecars in England before working for Pinewood Studios and built the state-of-the-art cars that James Bond drove in his last four movies.

Andy Smith. Photo by Cindy Goodman, North Shore News, *4228*

There are many residents who have been successful in all aspects of the movie and television industry, including computer animators James G. Hebb and Nicholas Boughen, both who have lengthy bios that include Emmy nominations.

Sports Associations and Teams

Mount Seymour Soccer Association: The association had its beginnings in 1961. Local fireman Dick Kenning cleared a hay field (later to become Myrtle Park) and began coaching local boys at soccer. Now part of the North Vancouver Football Club with NV Lions Gate Soccer and Lynn Valley Soccer Association, hundreds of players participate in weekend games at Seymour area parks and school fields.

North Shore Girls Soccer: Not to be outdone by the boys, girls soccer across Canada has become a hugely popular sport. The North Shore Girls Soccer Club is one of the largest sports clubs of any kind in Western Canada with approximately 3,500 players registered.

They are a community soccer club, providing girls and women on the North Shore with an opportunity to play soccer at many skill levels.

The club provides development opportunities for its players and coaches by supporting training programs, especially those delivered by the NSGSC Development Program and the North Shore

Soccer Development Centre. The new inside dome at Windsor school is a welcome change to playing in the rain.[84]

Mount Seymour Little League: Little league baseball has been around for a long time in Seymour. Recent presidents Rob Castagna and Tim Leclair and many volunteers were heavily involved in the club hosting the nationals in 2011. Mount Seymour Little League Division Five hosts teams for players from AAA (ages nine to eleven) to Big League (ages sixteen to eighteen).[85]

Some Community Associations

Imperial Order of Daughters of the Empire: Imperial Order of Daughters of the Empire (IODE) was founded in Canada in 1900. During the First World War the order was very active knitting socks for troops in the trenches overseas.

During the 1970s the Mount Seymour Chapter IODE was an active service club in the area. Local members included Mrs. Joan Ogden, Mrs. Rita Matsumoto, Mrs. Dolly George, Mrs. DuVerney, Mrs. Janet Pavlik, Mrs. L. Downie, Mrs. B. Sorochon and Mrs. A. Gardener.

The IODE was instrumental in providing health service equipment to northern Canadian communities and providing scholarships to university and college students.

Deep Cove Lions Club: The club was chartered in August 1999, sponsored by the Mount Seymour Lions Club. Guiding Lion was Gerry St. Laurent.

Deep Cove Lions is one of the few all-female Lions Clubs in the District. Some of its projects include popcorn at Concerts in the Park and other community

events, preparing lunches at the Parkgate Community Centre, catering for opening nights of theatre production and selling planters and hanging baskets for Mothers Day.

The Lions provide financial support for bursaries for students from Seycove and Windsor secondary schools. A few of the groups and organizations that have benefited from donations from the Lions over the years are: North Shore Safe House; North Shore Harvest House; BC Children's Hospital; North Shore Crisis Services Society; Easter Seal House; Lions Gate Hospital Foundation and BC Lions Society for Children with Disabilities.

Seymour Planning Association: Reference to the work of the association is made in the preface of this book. However, the efforts of many in the community cannot go unheralded.

In the early 1970s a group of concerned residents came together over major plans presented by the Grosvenor Plan to build "Seymour, a city in the suburbs" of 70,000. Ray Eagle of the Deep Cove Community Association together with Marilyn Baker and Don Bell, both of whom went on to become mayors of the District of North Vancouver (DNV), were part of a group that spearheaded the association. Their years of extensive research and public

CHRONOLOGY— GROUP UNITED AROUND RESPONSIBLE DEVELOPMENT (GUARD)

1970 The federal government sell the lands of the Blair Range to Canada Mortgage and Housing Corporation (CMHC) without informing the DNV

1971 Boy Scouts of Canada build the Baden Powell Trail, which was part of the Blair Range land. The DNV passes a motion that if any future development of this area were to occur, natural heritage must be preserved in the process

1994 70 ha (171.9 acres) of DNV land is rezoned for development of the Northlands Golf Course

1995 GUARD is established by four citizens concerned over the rezoning of DNV land and the proposal to build 2,150 new residences in Cove and Mountain forests

June 4 GUARD manages to gather 12,000 petition signatures against the proposed development

June 5 More than 400 people rally at the DNV council hall while Jim Cuthbert presents council with a motion to "amend bylaws to alter the land use designation for Cove and Mountain Forest from 'Urban Residential' to 'Parks, Recreation and Open Space'"

October 11 Public hearing in Windsor School on the upcoming DNV council vote

October 22 The DNV motion to rezone Cove and Mountain forest to Parks, Recreation and Open Space is ultimately passed six to one

questionnaires revealed the following aspirations of local residents:

> Preservation of Seymour's rural atmosphere;
>
> More shopping facilities in the form of separate village centres;
>
> A ban on more industrial developments;
>
> Minimum of multi-family housing and preference for medium high-rise apartments where necessary;
>
> More developed parkland, recreation facilities and public waterfront access;
>
> Division of the area into nine villages each with its own indigenous character;
>
> Improved public transportation;
>
> Strict control of future population increases.[86]

Luckily, today current district councils would likely agree to most of the above. Ray Eagle has prepared a history of the Seymour Planning Association and its activities, now housed in the Deep Cove Heritage Archives.

A 1971 census showed a population from the Seymour River to Indian Arm Inlet of approximately 11,000 people. The last census in 2006 showed close to 20,000.

Seymour Community Associations: In 1999 the East Seymour Community Association and the Roche Point Residents Association combined to form the Seymour Community Association. Other neighbourhood community associations in the area include the following: Seymour Valley Community Association; Blueridge Community Association; Indian Arm Ratepayers Association; Mount Seymour Parkway Community Association; Deep Cove Community Association; Inter-River Community Association; Maplewood Community Association; Panorama Drive Ratepayers Association; Strathcona Community Association; and the Woodlands Sunshine Cascade Ratepayers Association.

For details and contacts call Parkgate Community Services.

Policing and Emergency Services

North Shore Rescue: North Shore Rescue (NSR) is a volunteer-based search and rescue (SAR) team that provides life-saving services to the public of the Seymour area and beyond. Initially founded in September 1965, NSR is one of the oldest SAR teams in Canada. Its original mandate was to be a heavy urban SAR unit, used to assist with civil defence if a nuclear warhead detonated near Vancouver.

During its forty years of operation NSR has evolved into a SAR unit that focuses on mountain and urban helicopter rescue and public education. Over that time the team has seen more than 1,000 mountain SAR operations involving over 900 subjects and 53,000 hours of effort.

NSR was the first to develop and implement the Helicopter Flight Rescue System (HFRS). This technique sees trained members slung underneath a helicopter for lengths exceeding 200 feet to quickly access technical terrain and evacuate stranded or injured people. As well, NSR has installed comprehensive communication systems on the North Shore utilizing five strategically located VHF radio repeater sites. These are vital in rescue operations due to the mountainous terrain on the North Shore.[87]

North Shore Lifeboat Society (NSLS): The North Shore Lifeboat Society is a non-profit volunteer charity that owns, pays for and supports three all-weather marine search and rescue vessels, dedicated for use by the North Shore-based Canadian Coast Guard Auxiliary (CCGA).

North Shore Rescue, Auxiliary II. Photo by Robin Biggin, North Shore Rescue, 4439

The NSLS has been a registered charity since 1987 and was initially formed in response to marine incidents, which are inevitable with the high level of marine activity on the North Shore.[88]

Deep Cove lifeboat *Auxiliary II* is crewed by CCGA Pacific, Unit Two, and operates out of moorage provided by the Deep Cove Yacht club in North Vancouver.[89]

Canadian Coast Guard Auxiliary: The Canadian Coast Guard Auxiliary (CCGA) Pacific Region entails 29,500 kilometres (17,700 miles) of shoreline, 6,500 islands and approximately 450,000 sq km (174,000 sq mi) of internal and offshore waters. Its volunteers and vessels provide SAR response capability from forty-nine different units, one of which is Deep Cove.

On the North Shore the CCGA partners with the North Shore Lifeboat Society to provide an on-call response for marine emergencies in all seas and weather conditions. When a call-out is received the lifeboats are generally underway within twenty minutes with a complement of one coxswain and two to three crew members.[90]

BC Ambulance Service: Due to pressures from residents of the Seymour area, the DNV council arranged with BC Ambulance to establish an ambulance station at Kiwanis Care Centre on Burr place. The ambulance was finally stationed at this location in 2007.

Royal Canadian Mounted Police: Presently no community policing facility exists in the Seymour area. The North Vancouver detachment of the RCMP located at Sixteenth and Lonsdale polices the Seymour area. This includes a joint First Nations Task Force that works closely with the Tsleil-Waututh Nation.

North Vancouver District Firehall #4: It is interesting to note that the Deep Cove Volunteer Fire Brigade that was formed in the early 1940s became the embryo of the present DNV Fire Department. Armed with an antique man-powered hose reel, an assortment of brass nozzles and a goodly amount of community spirit, Ralph Bowditch, Frank Hamilton and Russ Kean were among the Cove volunteers.

Deep Cove Community Hall was home to the first Deep Cove fire truck.

Reg Smith headed up the volunteer fire brigade of locals. In 1953 the present DNV Fire Department was established and four firehalls in the District were formed.

The Seymour area was serviced by a firehall built in 1956 at 4805 East Keith Road, and in 1993 Deep Cove/Mount Seymour Firehall #4 was built on Mount Seymour Parkway to replace the old hall. The new fire station, nicknamed Hilton Hall for its superiority to the old hall, won an Award of Excellence design award from the DNV in 1994.[91]

Medical Services

Parkgate Community Health Centre: Many valuable resources on health care can be found on the second floor of the Parkgate Community Centre including information on senior and mental health services, immunization and parent–infant drop-in, meal services, chronic disease management programs and youth clinic.

RCMP Integrated First Nations police car. 4609

Physiotherapy

In 1987 Ross Ferry and Paige Larson founded Deep Cove Physiotherapy. Paige also founded North Shore Sports Medicine. Both clinics are located in the Dollar Shopping Centre. Paige works with Skate Canada and was chief therapist for Canadian figure skating at the 2010 Winter Olympics. They have two other locations, North Shore Winter Club and Capilano University.

Deep Cove's current firehall on Mount Seymour Parkway. 3734

CHRONOLOGY—DOCTORS

1948: The *North Arm Advertiser* advertises "Dr. McNeill Mon–Wed–Thur–Sat Mornings 11:00 am–12:00 pm telephone Deep Cove 2141 for appointment"

1950s Dr. Rueben's office is located at 56 Second Street in Deep Cove

1960s Dr. Shatzko opens second location in Dollar Shopping Centre

Dr. Curtis Latham and Dr. Jack Yasayko open part-time surgery on Gallant Avenue and carry patient files back and forth from their Lonsdale practices

1970s Dr. Bishop, Dollar Shopping Centre

Dr. Lyle Thurston and Dr. Paddy Mark open in renovated offices at Hanson Hardware on Deep Cove Road

1977 Dr. Rosemary Bason and Dr. Kay Sutherland, Dollar Shopping Centre

1978 Dr. Don Smith and Dr. Peter Richards renovate offices again

1978–79 Doctors Don Smith, Jim Wilde, A. Lee, David Hosgood and Peter Richards

1984 Doctors Peter Richards, Kay Sutherland and Rosemary Bason move to new building in Deep Cove at 4313 Gallant Avenue

1990 Doctors Richards, Maynard and Bergstrom open Park and Tilford Medical Clinic

2011 Doctors Peter Richards, Kay Sutherland, Wendy Loveless and Diane Barnett continue their practices on Gallant Avenue, treating the third generation of many local families

2011 Doctors Bergstrom, Lee, and Martin continue their practice at Parkgate Shopping Centre

Opposite bottom: Deep Cove Cabs, ca. 1960s. Courtesy Wayne Nemeth, 2360

CHRONOLOGY—PHARMACIES

1950s E.A. Worsley opens first pharmacy in Deep Cove

1970s Pharmasave opens in Dollar Shopping Centre

1984 Sheila, Ken and John Poon open Pharmacy on Gallant Avenue

1992 Safeway Pharmacy opens in Parkgate Shopping Centre

Shoppers Drug Mart opens in Parkgate Shopping Centre

2010 Rexall Deep Cove Pharmacy opens

Currently Seymour is happy to have the services of a good selection of doctors, dentists, chiropractors, optometrists and physiotherapists. The arrival of Life Labs a number of years ago is a great addition, although we are still missing X-ray facilities

Scouting

The motto of the 11th Seymour Scouts: There is no limit!

Scouting was originally founded in 1906 by Lord Robert Baden-Powell. Since that time Scouting has spread into a massive international movement in 216 countries. The 11th Seymour Scouts has been carrying out the Scouting mission in the Seymour area since 1947. In 2011 the 11th Seymour Scouts fell under the jurisdiction of the Scouts Canada Pacific Coast Council. The PCC was officially chartered on November 2, 2002, and subsequently re-chartered on May 1, 2004, by Scouts Canada.

Above left: Terry Tobin as a Boy Scout in the early 1950s. Courtesy Terry Tobin, 1680

Above right: Girl Guides in May Day Parade, 1954. Courtesy Joe Thornley, 0653

The 11th Seymour Scouts offer programs for all ages, including: Beavers (ages five to seven); Cubs (eight to ten); Scouts (eleven to fourteen, with option to remain until age sixteen); Venturers (fourteen to eighteen); and Rovers (eighteen to twenty-six).[92]

Guiding

In 1921 the first Guide groups were started in West Vancouver by Ruth Robinson and in North Vancouver by Gertrude and Dolly Barwise. The Seymour division was created in 1961 when the North Vancouver Girl Guides was divided into eight districts. Ten years later the Lions Area guiding division included three North Shore municipalities and communities from Squamish to Pemberton.[93] Guiding programs include Sparks (ages five to six), Brownies (seven to eight), Guides (nine to eleven), Pathfinders (twelve to fourteen) and Rangers (fifteen to seventeen).[94]

Transportation

Deep Cove Cabs: Founded in the 1940s by Alphonse Hauer, the cab company was an instant success. Due to the limited bus service people needed lifts in and out of the Cove and soon a second cab was added. The business sold twice, the second time to Hauers brother-in-law and sister Julius and Kay Nemeth, who operated it for many years.

Al Hauer of Deep Cove Cabs.
Courtesy Audry Hauer Rutledge, 2281

Buses: The story of the first bus service to operate from Deep Cove to downtown Vancouver is covered in *Echoes Across the Inlet.* Marge Buchanan recalls that "it took four buses to go anywhere from the Cove."

In 1973 a *Times* newspaper article reported on proposed cross-town buses for Mount Seymour Parkway and Dollarton Highway. Today, Coast Mountain Bus Company, a subsidiary company of Translink, operates regular half-hourly service to downtown Vancouver, with connections at Phipps Exchange to buses all over the North Shore.[95]

Community Awards

In 1993 several outstanding local citizens received medals presented by MP Chuck Cook to mark the 125th anniversary of Canadian Confederation. They included: Bill Cameron, who founded the Neil Squire Foundation in 1984 to increase independence of the severely disabled; Ernie Crist, long-time councillor for the District; Ken Fowler, president of Shaw Cable and head of the Canadian Cable Television Association; Sherrill Hardy, member of the Deep Cove Cultural Society board; Dudley Kill, who was involved in a number of North Shore service clubs including Mount Seymour Lions; and Arthur McLaren, president of Allied Ship Builders and one of North Vancouver's outstanding industrialists.

Politicians

The Seymour area has seen its fair share of politicians in the last forty years: Marilyn Baker, past mayor, Riverside; Ernie Crist, past councillor, Riverside; Mike Lakes, past councillor, Deep Cove; Doug MacKay-Dunn, present councillor, Indian River; Trevor Carolan, past councillor, Deep Cove; Verna Smelovsky, past councillor, Cove Cliff; Colin Gablemann, past MLA, North Vancouver–Cove Cliff; Jane Thornthwaite, present MLA, North Vancouver–Seymour; Lisa Muri, present councillor, Deep Cove; Heather Dunsford, past councillor, Deep Cove; Jim Cuthbert, past councillor, Indian River; and Naomi Yamamoto, current MLA for North Vancouver–Lonsdale.

Tourism

Seymour is a desirable destination for locals and tourists alike. The village charm of Deep Cove, the ski resort and wilderness recreation area on Mount Seymour and the public water access to sailing, boating, canoeing and kayaking all combine to make Seymour area an attractive tourist destination. There are no hotels in Seymour, the closest being the Holiday Inn on the west side of the Seymour River, but there is a good choice of first-class bed and breakfasts and excellent restaurants, plus a couple of neighbourhood pubs.

The Future of Seymour

BY JANET PAVLIK

Writers tell me that the wrap-up of a book is very important, but how do we finish the ongoing, ever-changing pattern of events that we have recorded on the previous pages? It is a difficult, if not impossible, challenge to foresee the future of Seymour.

Deep Cove resident Ray Eagle prepared the "Seymour Studies" report as a member of the Seymour Planning Association. Ray gives credit to the late Martin Chesworth, the District's then-senior planner, who led the project:

The Planning Department's studies emphasized most strongly that Seymour deserved special attention, and their main benefit was to provide a framework of thoughtful analysis. It is this analysis, to a large extent, that has shaped the Seymour we know today—not perfect, but most certainly better than it would be without having had this framework. The introduction to the first study, which examined the natural environment of Seymour, states: "The role of this study is to direct attention to natural

Cherry tree and view of Deep Cove, 2011. 4773

and physical attributes of the land . . . in this way we should avoid the problem of having to identify and compensate for conditions after a decision to develop has been made."

It is fortunate that the natural environment was quickly identified as the most important factor because that is the essence of Seymour. Remove that essence and it would become just another built-up area of no particular significance. In summing up this quandary, Martin Chesworth wrote in his inimitable way:

"For man, a love-hate relationship exists in this confrontation, where he imposes his suburban way of life upon the natural order, yet still cherishes contact with nature, for having cleared the forest he then attempts to reintroduce modified elements of nature by landscaping his suburban plot. This desire should constitute an important point of departure for our planning endeavour—in short, we must design with nature—at the community level, at the neighbourhood level, and at the level of the individual dwelling unit."

On talking with my thirteen-year-old grandson Brian Wilson, who lives in the Dollarton area (and who, after all, represents our future), he says he hopes the strong influence of the arts and culture in Seymour will continue. Windsor and Seycove Secondary schools have produced many talented students and he hopes that the future of Seymour remains on the edge of nature with a balance of wilderness and people living together.

Brian Wilson with First Light plaque, 2003. Photo by John Pavlik, 2950

Bios

Janet Pavlik

Born in London, England, in 1939 Janet (nee Gibbons) came to Regina, Saskatchewan, in 1961 to continue her career in the travel business. By 1962 she had completed a tour around the world for Burritt Travel and returned to Canada to write articles of her adventures and present a local TV travel show. Arriving in Vancouver to work for Alitalia Airlines in 1965, she met and married John Pavlik. In 1970 they settled in Deep Cove where they founded Pavlik Specialized Tours. They have lived there ever since.

Writing was something Janet always enjoyed and she started a weekly column on Deep Cove for the *Citizen* newspaper. From there her interest in local history was spiked—that story is told in the introduction to this book. In 1975 Janet took up the challenge of interviewing long-time residents of Deep Cove for a community TV series called *Early Days in Deep Cove.* By the 1980s she was writing a monthly travel column for the *Deep Cove Crier* newspaper. Participating in community affairs has always been a priority for the Pavliks.

Eileen Smith

Eileen grew up in and still lives in Deep Cove. Her paternal grandparents, maternal grandmother and parents had all made Deep Cove their homes beginning in the early 1940s. Eileen attended Burrard View and Windsor Secondary schools and was a member of the Mount Seymour Ski

Eileen Smith (left), Janet Pavlik and Desmond Smith. Photo by Michael Smith, 4621

Patrol for several years in the 1960s. She studied fine arts at the Three Schools of Art in Toronto and at Capilano College in the 1970s, which led her to photography in the 1980s. Eileen has been wandering around the Cove with a camera in her hand ever since.

Eileen worked for the *West End Times* and *Deep Cove Crier* as an ad layout artist for many years and now continues to write for the *Crier*. Eileen is a founding member of First Impressions Theatre and has produced over a hundred plays, musicals and concerts since 1983. She received the Don Marsh award for promoting harmony among community groups on the North Shore in 1986. Working for Deep Cove Heritage since 2001 has been a great joy to her and she is finally feeling justified in being a packrat by salvaging many of the photos, articles and tidbits for this book.

Desmond Smith

Desmond was born in Winnipeg, Manitoba, and moved to North Vancouver in 1954. He worked with the Air Services Branch of the government of Canada for nine years at its Pacific Regional headquarters and at Vancouver International Airport. After an extensive tour of Europe he joined the DNV where he worked for thirty-five years, first with the Engineering Department, then with the Land Department and finally with the Planning Department. As a member of the Canadian Institute of Planners he led the team that won the Award of Planning Excellence in Canada. He later wrote the first Official Community Plan for the DNV.

Left column from top: Janet Pavlik and Linda Moore, photo by Mike Wakefield, North Shore News, *3221; Connie Flett and Donna Serviss, photo John Pavlik, 2953; Guides receiving All Around Cord, courtesy Jenifer Bartlett, 3222; Terry Tobin kayaking, courtesy Genevieve Tobin, 4628. Middle column: Harvey Burt and Eric Morter, DCHS 1661; Deep Cove Ladies Lions with popcorn cart and friends, 4768; Les Petites Amis French Kindergarten, courtesy Madame Collette Mikhail, 4662; Jim Keayes and Jim Huzel, DCHS 2174. Right column: Dolly George, IODE member, DCHS 0001; Clara Bliss, 1987, DCHS 2158; Misha Wilson, 3293*

The Deep Cove Heritage Society has a collection of over 5,000 photos. Pictures and stories donated that did not appear in this book will be preserved in the archives. The group plans to have the archives online in the future. For more information visit the website:
deepcoveheritage.com

Some of Seymour's Street Names

Apex Avenue: Named after Apex–Alpine Provincial Park. It was originally planned to link with Mount Seymour Road but the decision to create Northlands Golf Course precluded this.

Banff Court: Originally planned as a through road, Banff Court is named after Banff National Park.

Belloc Street: Named after Hilaire Belloc, French-born British poet and member of Parliament (1870–1953).

Berkley Road and **Avenue:** Named after a very exclusive neighborhood in London's Mayfair. A very popular wartime song, sung by Vera Lynn, was *The Night a Nightingale Sang in Berkeley Square.*

Berton Place: Named after well-known Canadian author and broadcaster Pierre Berton (1920–2004). Berton wrote over fifty books on the history of Canada including *The National Dream, The Last Spike* and *Vimy*. Berton was awarded three Governor General's Awards for literature.

Birney Place: Named after Earle Birney, Canadian poet and writer of radio drama (1904–85). Birney won the Governor General's Award for *David and Other Poems*. His *Turvey: A Military Picaresque* won the Leacock Medal for Humour.

Bournemouth Crescent: Named after one of southern England's most beautiful towns where the Bourne River meets the sea.

Bowron Court: Named after a provincial park, as are Manning Crescent and Place, Nicolum Crescent, Nairn Court, Porteau Place and Ruckle Court.

Bridge Street: One of Seymour's earliest streets.

Brockton Crescent: Named after a ridge on Mount Seymour and the Chief Engineer of HMS *Plumper*, a survey vessel of the Royal Navy.

Bronte Drive: Named after the Bronte sisters, who wrote *Wuthering Heights, Agnes Grey* and *Jane Eyre*, among many other works.

Browning Place: Named after Elizabeth Barrett Browning, English poet (1806–61) later married to Robert Browning. Elizabeth Barrett Browning is best known for her romantic sonnets, especially "How Do I Love Thee?" (Let me count the ways . . .).

Byron Road and **Park:** Named after Baron George Gordon Byron, a leading British poet (1788–1824) who wrote "She Walks in Beauty" and "Don Juan." In the House of Lords he was a strong advocate of social reform.

Burr Place: Named after one of the first farmers in North Vancouver.

Burr supplied produce to the communities on Burrard Inlet and New Westminster. He was an ancestor of film and TV star Raymond Burr.

Carman Place: Named after Bliss Carman (1861–1929) the preeminent Canadian poet of his time, Carman was a writer and editor for the *Atlantic Monthly* and was noted for more than forty major works including "The Ships of Yule" (I saw three ships come sailing in. . .).

Carnaby Place: Yes, it was inspired by the Beatles!

Carnation Street: An older street named after flowers, including three sections named Violet Street.

Cummins Place: Named after an early merchant in Dollarton.

Dunrobin Place: Named by the developer after one of the best-known castles in Scotland.

Eddystone Crescent: Named after a famous lighthouse in southern England.

Ellis Street: Named after a pioneering family in western Seymour. Their lands eventually became part of the District of North Vancouver's Maplewood Farm.

Emerson Way and **Court:** Named after Ralph Waldo Emerson, American poet and essayist (1803–82), who was one of the great orators of all time.

Gallant Avenue: Gallant Avenue was originally a numbered street running down to the government wharf in Deep Cove. It was renamed to honour a popular local medical doctor, Dr. Gallant.

Garibaldi Drive and **Park:** Named after Garibaldi Provincial Park, which honours the founder of modern Italy.

Gaspe Place: Named after a provincial park on the Gaspe Peninsula in Quebec.

Goldie Court: Named after a small lake on Mount Seymour.

Golfing Names: Street names associated with golf courses are Caddy Road, Fairway Drive, Golf Drive and Glenhaven Crescent.

Ghmlye Drive: Located on the Tsleil-Waututh First Nation's land (Burrard Inlet Reserve).

Hardy Crescent: Named after Thomas Hardy, English novelist and poet (1840–1928). Hardy wrote many works including *Far from the Madding Crowd, The Return of the Native,* and *Tess of the d'Urbervilles.*

Hartford Place: Named by the developer after a New England city.

Hayseed Close: Named originally by the developer from Hayseed, Texas.

Hyannis Drive and **Point:** Named by the developer after Hyannis Port in New England.

Indian River Roads: Indian River Drive was surveyed by the province from North Vancouver to the top of the Indian Arm before the First World War, and constructed as far as Woodlands by the District. The roads built later, as part of the DNV Development Program are all named after features found along Indian Arm.

Keats Road: Named after John Keats, English poet (1795–1821) of the romantic era, who was a major influence to later famous poets. Among his best-known works are "Ode on a Grecian Urn" and "Ode to a Nightingale."

Lampman Place: Named after Archibald Lampman, Canadian poet (1861–99). Lampman was one of the so-called Confederation Poets, whose work focused on nature and rural life. He is considered one of Canada's finest poets.

Larkhall Crescent: Named after a town in southern Scotland overlooking the River Clyde. Best known for its ghost, the black lady of Larkhall.

Layton Drive: Named after poet Irving Layton. Born in Romania (1912–2006), Layton immigrated to Montreal in 1913. He was the first winner of the Governor General's Award for poetry.

Lima Road: Named after Sverre Lima, who emigrated from Norway in 1928. He bought property in the area with fellow Norwegian Gus Muri, as it reminded them of the Norwegian fjords. Butch and Arleen Lima still live there.

Loach Place: Named after land surveyor Tony Loach, who surveyed much of the recent development in Seymour for the District of North Vancouver.

Medwin Place: Named after Thomas Medwin (1788–1869), English poet and biographer of Shelley and Byron.

Mowat Place: Named after Farley Mowat, Canadian author (b.1921) and winner of the Governor General's Award. Mowat has written more than forty works including *The Regiment*, *Never Cry Wolf* and *The Dog Who Wouldn't Be.* He served as an intelligence officer with the Canadian Army during the Second World War in Sicily, Italy and the Netherlands.

Northlands Drive: Named after an early store and bus stop on Keith Road.

Panorama Drive and **Park:** Panorama Drive was originally the northern extension of Burns Avenue in Deep Cove. It was extended to the rock quarry and renamed to acknowledge the view it provided of the whole Cove.

Plymouth Drive: Named by the developer after the town in New England.

Riverside Drive: Riverside Drive is not an official street (rededicated provincial Crown land), but a right-of-way parcel of land owned by the municipality.

Shelley Road: Named after Percy Bysshe Shelley, English romantic poet (1792-1822). Shelley is recognized as a notable author of visionary poems such as "Prometheus Unbound" and a close friend and influence on Keats and Byron.

Swinburne Avenue: Named after Algernon Swinburne, English poet (1837–1909), who was considered by many as the successor to Tennyson and Robert Browning.

Takaya Drive: Named after the great wolf of the Tsleil-Waututh First Nation (Burrard Inlet Reserve).

Tollcross Road: Named after Tollcross Park in Glasgow, Scotland, renowned for its international rose garden, winter garden and secret garden.

Tompkins Crescent: Named in honor of Alice Tompkins, chief clerk of the Engineering Department, who served from the days of the District Engineer's inspections on horseback in the 1930s to the radio communications of the 1960s.

Walpole Crescent: Named after Sir Robert Walpole, regarded as the first prime minister of Great Britain (1676–1745).

Whitman Avenue: Named after Walt Whitman, American poet and essayist (1819–92). He was one of the favourite poets in the United States.

Wickenden Road and Park: Named after an early reeve of the District of North Vancouver.

Windsor Park: Named after the Queen's estate surrounding Windsor Castle.

Wyatt Place: Named after Sir Thomas Wyatt, English poet (1503–42). Wyatt was also advisor and ambassador in the service of King Henry VIII.

Sources

Chapter 1: Mount Seymour Alpine Area

1. *Mountain Mystery and History* (North Vancouver: Mt Seymour Resorts Limited, n.d.).
2. Ibid.
3. Ibid.
4. Alex Douglas, *The Mount Seymour History Project May 1997 Newsletter*, (North Vancouver: 1997).
5. Al Grass, Park Naturalist, Vancouver Natural History Society pamphlet, n.d.

Chapter 2: Indian Arm

6. "Indian Arm Provincial Park," BC Parks, accessed March 31, 2010, http://www.env.gov.bc.ca/bcparks/explore/parkpgs/indian_arm.
7. Tsleil-Waututh Nation. "Historic Provincial Park Management Plan Released." Press release, February 17, 2010, accessed May, 2012, http://www.twnation.ca/~/media/Files/Press%20Releases/TWN_PressRelease_SNKYCelebration.ashx.
8. "Indian Arm Provincial Park," BC Parks.
9. District of North Vancouver, *Indian Arm Development Review* (Envision Planning, 2009), accessed May 2012, http://www.dnv.org/upload/pcdocsdocuments/slw001!.pdf.
10. Ibid.
11. Indian Arm Natural History Group, *Map of Indian Arm*, North Vancouver, n.d.
12. District of North Vancouver, *Indian Arm Development Review.*
13. Eileen Stalker and Andrew Nolan, *Sea Kayak Paddling Through History: Vancouver & Victoria* (Surrey: Rocky Mountain Books, 2005), 94.
14. Indian Arm Natural History Group, *Map of Indian Arm.*
15. Stalker and Nolan, *Sea Kayak Paddling Through History.*
16. Indian Arm Natural History Group, *Map of Indian Arm.*
17. Cynthia Baxter, *Shadows of the Past at Frames Landing and Environs* (North Vancouver: printed by author, n.d.).
18. Ibid.
19. Indian Arm Natural History Group, *Map of Indian Arm.*
20. Stalker and Nolan, *Sea Kayak Paddling Through History.*

21. Say Nuth Khaw Yum/Indian Arm Provincial Park, *Park Management Plan*, Indian Arm Provincial Park Management Board, 22.
22. John McKay, "A Short History of Postal Service to Belcarra, Burrard Inlet & Indian Arm," *Belcarra Barnacle*, 1980.
23. Norman Hacking, "Floating Post Office Pioneer Dies at 92," *The Province*, April 2, 1976.
24. Patricia Eaton, "MV Scenic, Boat Brings Back Childhood Memories," *The Sunday News*, July 20, 1986.
25. Norman Hacking, "Floating Post Office Pioneer Dies at 92."
26. Ibid.
27. Marian Bruce, "Water-Borne Mail Route Ends 62-year Service," *Vancouver Sun*, October 31, 1970.

Chapter 3: Riverside East

28. Sharon Hogan, interview with the author, June 11, 2009.

Chapter 4: Maplewood

29. "Blueridge Creek Watershed Profile," The Pacific Streamkeepers Federation, accessed May 2012, http://www.pskf.ca/ecology/watershed/northvan/maplewood02.htm.
30. Bernardine Leong of Canexus Chemicals, email to the author, October 23, 2009.
31. ALS Group, *ALS New Vancouver Laboratory flyer*, September 2009.
32. "Blueridge Creek Watershed Profile," The Pacific Streamkeepers Federation.
33. Kevin Bell and Patricia M. Banning-Lover, *The Birder's Guide to Vancouver and the Lower Mainland*, Vancouver Natural History Society (Whitecap Books, 2001).

Chapter 5: Windridge

34. Martin Millerchip, "NVD Youth Centre Approved," *North Shore News*, May 26, 1991.
35. "About Chena," North Shore Chena Swim Team, accessed March 9, 2011, http://www.chenaswimclub.ca/SubTabGeneric.jsp?team=canscst&_stabid_=29299.
36. No author, "Parents Lobbying for Seymour Ice Arena," *Deep Cove Crier*, February 1993.
37. "North Shore – About us," Canlan Ice Sports webpage, accessed May 2012, http://www.icesports.com/northshore/about-us.aspx.
38. Seymour Dance, accessed May 2012, http://www.seymourdance.com/Home.html.

39. "Darren Perkins – Biography," Darren Perkins, accessed July 13, 2009, http://darrenperkins.ca/bio.

Chapter 6: Seymour Heights

40. *School Plan for 2010-2011: Seymour Heights Elementary School*, North Vancouver School District, 2010, accessed May 2012, http://www.nvsd44.bc.ca/~/media/CB3E225FC60B42C0B-CA4E849301F8F63.ashx.

41. "Seymour Heights PAC," Seymour Heights Parent Advisory Council (PAC), accessed May 2012, http://www.seymourheight-spac.com.

Chapter 7: Blueridge

42. *School Plan for 2011-2012: Blueridge Elementary*, North Vancouver School District, 2011, accessed May 2012, http://www.nvsd44.bc.ca/~/media/Schools/BL%202011-12%20School%20Plan.ashx.

43. Ibid.

44. "Good Neighbour Day," Blueridge Community Association, accessed May 2012, http://members.shaw.ca/blueridgeca/Good%20Neighbour%20Day.htm.

45. Betty Carrington, "If You Go down to the Woods Today," *The Blueridge Community News*, April, 2009.

46. "The Robeez Story," Stride Rite, accessed August 4, 2010, http://www.robeez.com/en-us/about/sandra.htm.

Chapter 8: Windsor Park

47. *School Plan 2009 – 2010: Plymouth Elementary School*, North Vancouver School District, 2009, accessed May 2012, http://www.nvsd44.bc.ca/~/media/FA6A7F59A24048D4BC-056E1720C5D631.ashx.

48. "District of North Vancouver Parks," Corporation of the District of North Vancouver, accessed May 2012, http://www.dnv.org/article.asp?c=419.

Chapter 9: Tsleil-Waututh Nation

49. "About TWN: Our Future," Tsleil-Waututh Nation, accessed November 29, 2010, http://www.twnation.ca/en/About%20TWN/Our%20Journey/Our%20Future.aspx.

Chapter 11: Northlands

50. Memorandums and Personal correspondence of Lieutenant-Colonel R.M. Blair V.D., from 1st Battalion, Seaforth Highlanders of Canada, City of Vancouver Archives, Vancouver, BC.

Chapter 12: Parkgate

51. *United Church 10th Anniversary* (North Vancouver: Mount Seymour United Church, 1999).

52. *United Church 1937-1976 History* (North Vancouver: Mount Seymour United Church, n.d., ca. 1976).

53. Archives at North Vancouver District Library, Parkgate branch, North Vancouver, BC.

Chapter 13: Parkway

54. *Cedar Springs Retirement Residence – A Natural Fit* (North Vancouver: Pacific Arbour Retirement Communities, n.d.).

55. "Mount Seymour Lions Club History," Mount Seymour Lions Club, accessed September 11, 2011, http://www.mountseymour-lions.org/club/history.

Chapter 14: Indian River

56. *School Plan for 2011-2012: École Dorothy Lynas Elementary*, North Vancouver School District, accessed May 2012, www.nvsd44.bc.ca/~/media/Schools/DorothyLynas/About%20Our%20School/DL%202011-12%20School%20Plan%20Revised.ashx.

Chapter 15: Roche Point

57. Tsleil-Waututh Nation and the District of North Vancouver, *Cates Park/Whey-ah-Wichen Park Master Plan and Cultural Resources Interpretation Master Plan* (North Vancouver: May, 2006), accessed May 2012, http://www.dnv.org/upload/pcdocsdocuments/xp01!.pdf.

58. "About Us," North Vancouver – Save Our Shores Society, accessed March 16, 2011, http://www.nv-saveourshores.ca/AboutUs/tabid/54/Default.aspx.

59. Tsleil-Waututh Nation and the District of North Vancouver, *Cates Park/Whey-ah-Wichen Park Master Plan.*

60. Allan Orr, "Roche Point Forest: A Community Resource in Limbo," *The Seymour Eagle*, n.d.

61. Donald A. Blood, *Wildlife in British Columbia at Risk: The Pacific Water Shrew* (Victoria: Province of British Columbia Ministry of Environment, Lands and Parks, 1995), accessed May 2012, http://www.env.gov.bc.ca/wld/documents/shrew.pdf.

62. Marry Huntington, "Give Eagle a Chance in NVD," *North Shore News*, November 29, 1987.

63. Paul Houle, "Girl Guides Continue NVD Eagle Nest Fight," *North Shore News*, October 25, 1987.

64. *CBC News*, "Mutilated Eagles Found in North Vancouver," February 3, 2005.

Chapter 16: Dollarton

65. *School Plan 2011-2012: L'école Sherwood Park School*, North Vancouver School District, 2011, accessed May 2012, http://www.nvsd44.bc.ca/~/media/Schools/SherwoodPark/PDFs/SP%202011-12%20School%20Plan%202%20posted%20to%20website.ashx.

66. "Sherwood Park - French Immersion," North Vancouver School District, accessed October 2011, http://www.nvsd44.bc.ca/SchoolSites/SherwoodPark/About_Us/French_Immersion.aspx.

67. Grace Moul, *The First Fifty Years Seymour Golf and Country Club Book* (North Vancouver: printed by Seymour Golf and Country Club, n.d.).

68. Mike Inwood, "'Unique' teacher calls it quits and heads into bush," *Deep Cove Crier*, July 1995.

Chapter 17: Cove Cliff/Strathcona

69. Les Rimes, "Action on Deep Cove Dam," *The Vancouver Times*, February 25, 1965.

70. "Deep Cove PPP: History," Deep Cove Parent Participation Preschool, accessed February 24, 2011, http://www.deepcoveppp.com/About_Us/History.

71. Stella Jo Dean, letter to the editor, *North Shore News*, June 1, 1980.

72. No author, "Anglican church gets new name," *Deep Cove Crier*, May, 2007.

73. "The Muri Family, True Pioneers of Deep Cove," District of North Vancouver Community Heritage Commission Newsletter, n.d.

74. E. E. Rand & Fowler, Letter to Robert Stirrat, July 29, 1947.

Chapter 18: Deep Cove

75. Ian Noble, "North Van house fire claims a life," *North Shore News*, May 3, 1995.

76. John Hutchinson, "DCYC Club History," email to the author, May 14, 2008.

77. Deep Cove Clearwater Committee, *Report on Future Marine Development in Deep Cove*, North Vancouver, June 1979.

78. Ibid.

79. Deep Cove Cultural Society, *Deep Cove Cultural Centre, an Arts Development Project*, (North Vancouver: sponsored by the Corporation of the District of North Vancouver, 1988).

80. Ibid.
81. Trevor Carolan, "Heritage warrior Bill Blakely passes at 70," *Deep Cove Crier*, September 1996.
82. "About Us," Neil Squire Society, accessed March 17, 2011, http://www.neilsquire.ca/about.
83. Frances Gray, "Independence urged, Deep Cove for Separation," *Citizen*, April 1, 1977.

Chapter 19: Multicommunity

84. "About NSGSC," North Shore Girls Soccer Club, accessed December 8, 2011, http://www.nsgsc.ca.
85. "Mt. Seymour Little League: Mount Seymour 2011 Divisions," Mount Seymour Little League, accessed December 8, 2011, http://www.eteamz.com/msll/divisions.
86. "Seymour: an assembly of village," *Times of North and West Vancouver*, September 6, 1973.
87. "About Us – North Shore Rescue," North Shore Rescue Team Society, accessed March 3, 2011, http://www.northshorerescue.com/about-us.
88. "North Shore Lifeboat Society: About Us," North Shore Lifeboat Society, accessed March 26, 2011, http://www.northshorelifeboat.ca.
89. "Our Lifeboats," North Shore Lifeboat Society, accessed March 26, 2011, http://www.northshorelifeboat.ca/index-2.html.
90. "Canada Coast Guard Auxiliary – Pacific – About," Canada Coast Guard Auxiliary Pacific Region, accessed March 3, 2011, http://www.ccga-pacific.org/ccga-p/about.php.
91. *New Associate Editor Dave Dean Rings a Bell* (North Vancouver: 1964), North Vancouver Museum and Archives, North Vancouver, BC.
92. 11th Seymour Scouts Facebook page, accessed March 22, 2011, http://www.facebook.com/pages/11th-Seymour-Scouts/91271189380#!/pages/11th-Seymour-Scouts/91271189380?sk=info.
93. Maureen Rennie, *Tracing Lions Heritage, History of Girl Guiding in Lions Area BC 1921-2001* (Girl Guides of Canada, Lions Area Council, 2002).
94. Girl Guides of Canada, accessed March 22, 2011, http://www.girlguides.ca.
95. Coast Mountain Bus Company, accessed December 14, 2011, http://www.coastmountainbus.com.

Planning Reports—
District of North Vancouver (DNV)

1963	“Prospects of Growth”, DNV Planning Department
1963	“Parks 63”, DNV Planning & Parks Departments
1964	“Plan 64”, DNV Planning Department
1970	“A Development Study…”, Grosvenor International, for DNV
1975	“Seymour 1, the Natural Environment”, DNV Planning Department
1975	“Seymour 2, the Existing Neighbourhood”, DNV Planning Department
1977	“Seymour 1A, Maplewood Estuaries”, DNV Planning Department
1977	“Development of Seymour”, the council of the DNV to staff
1983	“Maplewood Official Community Plan”, Bylaw 5552
1983	“Seymour Development Plan”, DNV Planning Department
1984	“Alpine Area Background Report”, DNV Planning Department
1985	“Seymour Official Community Plan”, Bylaw 5815
1985	“Panorama-Deep Cove Park Design”, Diamond, Guzzi, Perry, Wuoi, for DNV
1986	“Alpine Area Official Community Plan”, Bylaw 5800
1989	“Echoes Across the Inlet”, Deep Cove and Area Association
1990	“District of North Vancouver Official Community Plan”, DNV Planning Department
1995	“Deep Cove to Dollarton Waterfront”, DNV Waterfront Task Force
1999	“The Waterfront Task Force”, DNV Phase 2
2004	“The Maplewood Project”, Eco-Industrial-Sustainable Planning, DNV
2004	“Seymour Local Plan”, Bylaw 7347

Bibliography

Bell, Kevin and Patricia M. Banning-Lover. The Birder's Guide to Vancouver and the Lower Mainland, by the Vancouver Natural History Society. Vancouver: Whitecap Books, 2001.

Blood, Donald A. Wildlife in British Columbia at Risk: The Pacific Water Shrew. Victoria: Province of British Columbia Ministry of Environment, Lands and Parks, 1995. http://www.env.gov.bc.ca/wld/documents/shrew.pdf.

Deep Cove Clearwater Committee. Report on Future Marine Development in Deep Cove. North Vancouver: published by the Deep Cove Clearwater Committee, 1979.

Deep Cove Cultural Society. Deep Cove Cultural Centre, an Arts Development Project. North Vancouver: sponsored by the Corporation of the District of North Vancouver, 1988.

District of North Vancouver. Indian Arm Development Review. Envision Planning, 2009. http://www.dnv.org/upload/pcdocsdocuments/slw001!.pdf.

Douglas, Alex. "Mountain Mystery and History." Program description published by Mt Seymour Resorts Limited, North Vancouver, n.d.

Indian Arm Natural History Group. "Map of Indian Arm." North Vancouver: n.d. Illustration by Liz Shelton.

Moul, Grace. The First Fifty Years Seymour Golf and Country Club Book. North Vancouver: printed by Seymour Golf and Country Club, n.d.

North Vancouver School District. School Plan 2009 – 2010: Plymouth Elementary School. Last modified November 5, 2009. Approved by Dave Pearce, Assistant Superintendent NVSD44. http://www.nvsd44.bc.ca/~/media/FA6A7F59A24048D4BC056E1720C5D631.ashx.

Stalker, Eileen and Andrew Nolan. Sea Kayak Paddling Through History: Vancouver & Victoria. Surrey: Rocky Mountain Books, 2005.

Stevenson, John. Songs of Indian Arm: a tribute in poetry. Swansea: Eyecatchers, 1995.

Tsleil-Waututh Nation and the District of North Vancouver. Park Master Plan and Cultural Resources Interpretation Master Plan. North Vancouver: May, 2006. http://www.dnv.org/upload/pcdocsdocuments/xp01!.pdf.

United Church 10th Anniversary. North Vancouver: Mount Seymour United Church, 1999.

United Church 1937-1976 History. North Vancouver: Mount Seymour United Church, n.d., ca. 1976.

Index